MW01001555

too good
to be true

finding hope in a world of hype

too good
to be true
finding hope in a world of hype

michael horton

GRAND RAPIDS, MICHIGAN 49530 USA

Too Good to Be True
Copyright © 2006 by Michael Horton

Requests for information should be addressed to:

Zondervan, *Grand Rapids, Michigan 49530*

Library of Congress Cataloging-in-Publication Data

Horton, Michael Scott.
 Too good to be true : finding hope in a world of hype / Michael Horton.
  p. cm.
 Includes bibliographical references.
 ISBN-10: 0-310-26745-5
 ISBN-13: 978-0-310-26745-4
 1. Suffering—Religious aspects—Christianity. 2. Consolation.
 3. Hope—Religious aspects—Christianity. 4. Jesus Christ—Crucifixion.
 5. Jesus Christ—Resurrection. I. Title.
 BV4909.H67 2006
 248.8'6—dc22

                                                                    2005031943

This edition printed on acid-free paper.

Interior design by Michelle Espinoza

Printed in the United States of America

06 07 08 09 10 11 12 • 18 17 16 15 14 13 12 11 10 9 8 7 6 5 4 3 2 1

*To Linda Bossman, Judith Riddell, the Mebergs,
and the Duguid family for being God's "masks"*

contents

part one:
GOD of the cross

chapter one
when tragedy strikes

I felt as if I were a willful teenager again, with my father shaking me by the shoulders to bring me to my senses. Only now, he could not grab me. He could not even speak to me, although he desperately mumbled strange sounds. All that was left of the man were his eyes, pounding against my heart with their steely gray intensity.

As everyone who knew him even casually could attest, my father had eyes that laughed before the rest of his face could catch up. Some of us, especially his children, knew that, on those rare occasions when his temper flared, it happened first in his eyes. With a mere glance, he could nip horseplay in the bud at the dinner table. Now those eyes were almost always reporting an emotion we had never seen in our dad. The one for whom the glass was always half full, who always landed on his feet in every circumstance, was more terrified of waking than of dying.

Have you ever seen someone wail without actually being able to articulate a cry, his heaving chest and terrified visage giving the secret away? Larger than life since my childhood, this great man was now as helpless as an infant and more pitiful than any life I had ever known, his gaunt flesh wasting and yellowing with every passing week.

At the age of seventy-eight, James Horton had been diagnosed with a benign brain tumor that required immediate surgery. At first, a shunt released some of the fluid on his brain, but a further surgery was necessary to excise the rapidly growing lump before it interrupted vital brain functions. This surgery failed, and before long we realized that my father would not recover.

He lived for nearly a year, however, almost paralyzed from head to toe. Since even his face had lost muscular control, his eyelids drooped, exposing their red interior. It was as if his whole face had melted like wax, and we could hardly recognize him — except for the eyes, which were always filled with emotion, usually unspeakable pain. But occasionally, and more frequently toward the end, they evidenced hope and a confidence that came from another place.

We prayed for weeks that the Lord would take him home. We would place our son, just a few months old, in his namesake's listless arms and watch my dad's heaving chest signal his delight. Even then, it was always a bittersweet visit for my father, and for us.

The Gibraltar of the family, my mother, fussed over his bedside, nervously fluffing his pillows at fifteen-minute intervals, ensuring that the intravenous fluids were properly calculated, and organizing edifying visits from friends and children from church. In between, she read quietly in her chair while holding Dad's hand. For years, I had witnessed the remarkable care that these two people provided in our home, first to their own parents and then to fifteen elderly folks in our residential care home as I was growing up. But now she was caring for her best friend, and there was almost nothing she could do for him but fluff his pillows — and try to hide her own daily grief. Although my mom always looked ten years younger than her actual age, these months acted like time-lapse photography, working my father's pain into her own face and wearing her body down.

A Second Blow

Then, just two months before my father's death, Mom suffered a massive stroke while I was driving her from her sister's funeral, where she had delivered a moving eulogy. This strong and compassionate woman who had given her life to disadvantaged city kids and abandoned seniors was now herself dependent on others.

I recalled a couple of times in the past when my parents had mentioned their worst fears about old age. For my dad, a debilitating disease would be the most horrible way of death, he said; for my mom, it was being a burden—and from their caregiving experience they knew both well. In my darker moments, I wondered why God would allow them to experience their worst scenarios in the last act of their play, especially when they had done so much for so many others. They had moved close to Lisa and me in our first year of marriage to be of help when they learned of our first pregnancy. Always running to the side of those who needed a strong arm, my mom was now partially paralyzed and disabled, while my dad was succumbing to an agonizing death.

I told God that it all seemed *too* calculated, that he seemed all *too* real, *too* involved, *too* present in our lives, especially my parents', as if he had cruelly dished out the very end that each most feared. Shouldn't people whose lives were all about giving to others, especially to the elderly, have a break when it comes to how *they* leave this life? It seemed to challenge the whole "reap what you sow" principle: does this apply only when people deserve bad and not when they deserve good?

My wife, recovering from several especially difficult miscarriages, found that her visits to my dad's bedside only aggravated her questions about God's goodness. It was strange to see her go through this. After all, Lisa was a Bible study teacher who devoured pretty deep theology books. Now it was all being put to the test of real life.

I had experienced death up close in our home growing up, not only with my grandparents but also with the adopted "grandparents" in our home for the elderly. Still, Lisa and I both struggled with the usual doubts. People suffer and even die from natural causes every day, we tried to tell ourselves. Furthermore, old people eventually die. We all die. This doesn't mitigate the tragedy, but its inevitability and universality at least prepare us for the *fact*.

But why do some people suffer so much in their death? Why is it often so slow and painful? Is *death* itself not horrible enough that we also have to fear *dying*—a wasting and withering that threatens our cherished expectations of a good and orderly providence? Just to look at my father over the course of those ghastly months, those long and torturous weeks, was to face the most serious, existential, concrete challenges to our deeply held Christian convictions.

Marching to Zion . . . OK, *Limping*

Years after maneuvering to inherit his brother's birthright, Jacob received word that Esau was on his way to meet him. (The story is told in Genesis 32–33). This was not good news of a family reunion but a harbinger of certain war between what were now two sizable camps, and Jacob was deeply disturbed, so he prayed and reaffirmed his faith in God's covenant promise. Sending a farmyard of livestock ahead of him as a gift, Jacob hoped to placate his brother's anger.

That night, however, Jacob is ambushed not by his brother but by a strange man who is identified with no less than God himself. In this unexpected wrestling match, Jacob is allowed to "win" and as a result receives the Lord's blessing: the Lord makes himself weak in order to deliver the promise by grace, accommodating himself to the feebleness of his covenant servant. Yet Jacob walks away from the scene with a limp that he carries with him throughout his life—a groin injury that pointed to the promise and the perils of being an heir of promise, a child of Jacob, now renamed "Israel." As dangerous as it was to meet face-to-face with his angry brother, Jacob realized that he had encountered a greater foe on the battlefield and had prevailed, by the grace of the enemy, who was really his friend.

It is, of course, true that "all's well that ends well," as Shakespeare's title has it. Today, my father is no longer suffering even the ordinary vicissitudes of daily life; he is in the presence of the triune God, awaiting with us the resurrection of the body. Yet even in the trial itself there was a calm in the middle of the storm. In fact, it wasn't really a calm, but a deep, moving current of Spirit-given life drawn from Immanuel's veins.

When it came to faith, my dad was the strong, silent type. A hard worker raised during the Depression, he had always been a scrapper whose hands were worn from labor, not from turning pages. Although my father was an entertaining storyteller, my mother nurtured my faith and my interest in reading, studying, and asking questions. Yet against the bleak backdrop of death we witnessed a swelling confidence in God's grace and goodness that my father had not always displayed. In between dark days of despair, when his eyes seemed to scream at us, *Make it end!* there were moments of genuine joy in the cross and resurrection, as Scripture was read or the elements of Communion were placed in his mouth, or when children sang songs of Zion. He would lift his forefinger as far "north" as he could muster, pointing to the Wellspring of his hope. Even as his flesh was wasting, he was being renewed inwardly.

It was as if the process of sanctification was keeping pace with the process of physical decay. Nothing happening to him physically gave him hope, but he was being inwardly renewed in the hope of soon meeting his God and then, at the last, experiencing the glorious life of a reunited soul and body, free of sin and pain.

Stressful months still followed at our house, with a toddler and then triplets (who barely survived their three-month-premature delivery). One spent his first four months in intensive care and, as I write (he's two now), has just returned from another stint in ICU after being severely injured while playing. These events remind us time and again that life is both a tragedy and a comedy, often at the same time. Martin Luther said that the baker is God's mask, providing us daily bread. Similarly, countless doctors, nurses, brothers and sisters from church and seminary, friends near and far, not to mention literally thousands whom we will never meet and yet who included us in their prayers, have been God's own means of wrapping us in his arms and reassuring us that he cares for our loved ones—and for us as well, more tenderly and wisely than we do ourselves. A fellow pastor who successfully came through cancer treatment expressed the same overwhelming joy in discovering the concrete presence of Christ through his body. "People I've never met sent me letters and picked me up for doctors' appointments," he said. "It's amazing!"

Our weaknesses really are an opportunity for God to show his strength. This isn't just a platitude. Another interesting point Luther made was that being a theologian of the cross—which is the general vocation of every Christian—requires three things: *oratio* (prayer), *meditatio* (study), and *tentatio* (trials). It is pretty easy to reduce faith to a "peaceful, easy feeling" of uplifting prayer and praise ("Just pray about it," according to the sometimes glib advice of our Christian subculture). It's also easy to turn faith into mere assent — a merely academic exercise concerned simply with getting the answers right on the exam. If we just memorize enough Scripture and quote it at the right moments, we'll be fine; or if we just get our theology right, everything else will fall into place. Yet without the *trials*, faith is not really roused to grab hold of the God of promise.

In a moving and sympathetic exchange of correspondence, John Calvin once told Cardinal Sadoleto that what the prelate needed most in order to understand that all of his righteousness before God was Christ's and in no measure his own was a crisis of conscience. He needed to be shaken in his confidence that he could cooperate with God's grace sufficiently to attain a final acquittal. Trials come in all sizes and shapes, targeting our conscience, our hopes and dreams, our expectations of how life works, our confidence in God and his purposes. Lisa and I have had our faith tested; and although we are even less confident in the future on its own terms, we are more confident in the God who holds it, and us, in his hand. The trials do make a difference.

But precisely because life is both tragedy and comedy, it is more apparent to us than ever that our hearts are fickle. When life goes well, we wonder how it could be better ("Sure, the manna is okay, but can he give us meat?"). When things head south, we challenge God's fatherly care ("Did he bring us into this desert to die?").

On one side are counselors so concerned to clear God of charges that they underplay the element of complaint to which even the psalmist gave eloquent voice — the blues of the Bible. On the other side are those who sentimentalize suffering and defend the sufferer at the expense of the only One whose sovereignty and goodness can provide transcendent solace. Sufferers do not need to be told they ought to rejoice without raising complaints to their God. But they are no better served when their trials are treated as a referendum on God's existence or character.

For the most part, God surrounded us with better counselors by far than Job's and—what we often need most when going through trials—with good ears. Listening is an art that I've grown to appreciate as I have seen it modeled in wise saints.

Preparing for the Test

Where all of this leads is to a conviction that learning theology is very difficult to do in the trial itself. It is not a good time for being taught. The wounds are too open to the elements. This doesn't mean it *cannot* be done, but it is more difficult, at least for many.

Even comforting truths can be an irritation when our nerves are raw. Understanding who God is, who we are, and God's ways in creation, providence, and redemption—at least as much as Scripture reveals to us—is to the trials of life what preparing for the LSAT is to the practice of law. Theology is the most serious business. Preparing for this exam is not just a head game or a prerequisite for a temporal vocation, but it's a matter of life and death. It is about our heavenly vocation and its implications for each day here and now. It's about living, and dying, well.

The reason I have reflected on these fairly fresh events in my own experience is not to record an autobiography but to give a preface, and even a context, for the approach to suffering and hope that we will glean from Scripture in the following chapters. We don't all suffer in the same way, and there are no Congressional Medals for trials, no "Sufferer of the Year" awards. While we can rank suffering when standing outside of it, it is all pretty relative when we are a part of it. Furthermore, while physical and spiritual suffering are at least to some degree intertwined, it is not always in the same degree for every person.

To this day, my mother has not struggled with God's mysterious ways as much as I have, even though her physical and emotional pain has been immeasurably greater. Within the scope of weeks, she had lost her closest sister (also to a stroke) and her husband, and had experienced a series of strokes that left her paralyzed on one side and unable to speak. The doctors told us that, while ordinary strokes can be like seeds in a watermelon, a massive stroke like hers was more like lopping off a third of the melon; and although she still had her wits about her, they had little confidence that she would ever walk or speak again. Not the type to take such counsel seriously, my mom was resolved to pursue rehabilitation aggressively. As I write nearly three years after the stroke, she can walk with assistance and care for many of her personal needs with her left hand. While her speech is often garbled, and she often cannot say what she is thinking, her frustration is veiled in self-deprecating humor and gratitude to God for all the recovery he has given her. Although she had to suddenly surrender her independence—apartment, car, and familiar environment—the confidence in God's goodness and sovereignty that she taught and exhibited throughout her life remains the wellspring of her outlook and a powerful witness to the rest of us. Life for her is different now—in some ways worse, bereft of past comforts and cherished loves, but in other ways sweeter, with grandchildren competing with each other for a spot on her lap. "Besides," she says, "I can still read my Bible."

"All that God does is right" may sound like an unwelcome or Stoic resolve that has not yet felt the full force of life's blows, but I can hardly attribute that to Mom. Perhaps it is because she has suffered more and cared so long for those who suffer that, as one hymn has it, the "solid joys and lasting treasures" of Zion are so palpably close to her experience. Maybe differing personalities play a role as well. While God is infinitely so, even we are mysteries to ourselves.

Sometimes we suffer for righteousness' sake, other times for our own folly, and quite often, simply as a result of belonging to a fallen creation in which suffering and death are inevitable. They twist everything that God made straight, distort all he created in wisdom, and disfigure that which was beautiful. Regardless of the diversity our trials take, one thing is certain: we will all suffer. Even if we do not have a lot of sound teaching to fall back on, we can be comforted by the truth of God's grace in the middle of it all and learn, or be reconfirmed in, a few marvelous promises, even in the valley of the shadow of death.

The experience of suffering itself does not make us experts on the subject. Golfing *more* will not correct one's bad swing; only training can do that. And so we need to learn from God's Word how to meet trials, apart from which *more* tough times will only tend to reinforce what we already believe, whether it's good or bad theology.

Many readers will have endured far deeper and more lasting difficulties than our family has. But we all have something to bring to the table from our own experience in this matter. More important, we all have the Scriptures, which can critique and interpret our experience in a godly and productive way. I am not qualified to write this book because of the degree of suffering I've encountered, which is undoubtedly slight in comparison to many readers of this book. Rather, these events, and others I will recount throughout the various chapters, have simply brought home in fresh and vital ways the truths of God's Word that have been an enormous comfort to our family and to Christians down through the ages.

These chapters are intended to be relevant to the whole spectrum of trials: physical pain; emotional distress; being wronged by others; and our own sin, doubts, and spiritual depression.

Wherever the reader is located in life's circumstances and shaped by God's hand in nature and nurture, may the devotional exercises in this study be both a balm in the middle of trials and a study guide for the exam of life.

chapter two
good news for losers

The Christian movement is a degeneracy movement composed of reject and refuse elements of every kind.... It is therefore not national, not racially conditioned; it appeals to the disinherited everywhere; it is founded on a rancor against everything well-constituted and dominant: it needs a symbol that represents a curse on the well-constituted and dominant. It also stands in opposition to every spiritual movement, to all philosophy: it takes the side of idiots and utters a curse on the spirit. Rancor against the gifted, learned, spiritually independent: it detects in them the well-constituted, the masterful....

Dionysus [the god of revelry who was cut in pieces] versus the "Crucified": there you have the antithesis. It is not a difference in regard to their martyrdom — it is a difference in the meaning of it.... The god on the cross is a curse on life, a signpost to seek redemption from life; Dionysus cut to pieces is a promise of life: it will be eternally reborn and return again from destruction.

Friedrich Nietzsche, *The Will to Power*

We don't like to think of ourselves as losers, especially in America. Even popular religion is often exploited in what Friedrich Nietzsche would celebrate as "the will to power." If it is going to sell in the marketplace, it must be clearly seen that our particular brand of religion will make us winners in business and politics, boost our self-confidence, and position us and our families as the envy of our non-Christian neighbors. In part, this is an attempt to answer the claim that religion in general, but Christianity in particular, is for the weak. A contemporary of ours who embodies Nietzsche's will to power (and his appraisal of Christianity) is media mogul Ted Turner, who, though raised in a conservative Christian background, now reportedly calls Christianity "a religion for losers."[1]

How do you react when you read these words or encounter them in veiled remarks by friends, coworkers, and relatives who do not know Christ? For at least a century and a half, American evangelism has spent great effort and money on public relations campaigns for Christianity in just this area of concern. Famous athletes, politicians, entertainers, and other icons of popular culture are regularly trotted out as trophies of grace. Have you ever seen a janitor interviewed for his testimony?

Of course, there are notable exceptions, such as Joni Eareckson Tada, who has brought so much wisdom to suffering since her diving accident left her paralyzed. But we seem obsessed at times with convincing the world that we are cool, which especially in this culture means healthy, good-looking, prosperous, and, even better, famous. Not only can one remain cool in Christ; it is this personal relationship with Jesus that, far from calling us to die, gives us that little bit extra to "be all we can be." At least that's what the before-and-after testimonies seem to suggest. Jesus came to recruit a team of all-stars and coach them to the Super Bowl of better living.

Any Place for Weakness?

How do we square all this with Jesus' statement that "those who are well have no need of a physician, but those who are sick. I have not come to call the righteous but sinners to repentance" (Luke 5:31 – 32)? Paul also gives a recurring emphasis to weakness: "On my own behalf I will not boast, except of my weaknesses.... But [the Lord] said to me, 'My grace is sufficient for you, for my power is made perfect in weakness.' Therefore I will boast all the more gladly of my weaknesses, so that the power of Christ may rest upon me. For the sake of Christ, then, I am content with weaknesses, insults, hardships, persecutions, and calamities. For when I am weak, then I am strong" (2 Corinthians 12:5, 9 – 10). Would Paul have made a very good spokesman for "muscular Christianity" or for the other images of success so widely praised among us?

In his *Varieties of Religious Experience* (1902), Harvard philosopher William James distinguished between two types of religion: "healthy-minded" and "morbid-minded," which he also called the religion of the "sick soul." Those who belong to the sick-soul camp, he said, see themselves as sinful, dispossessed, and disinherited, while the healthy-minded exude optimism. America has attracted the disinherited of the earth to our shores in order to make a better life for themselves and their posterity. It's one of the amazing gifts we have: to "pull ourselves up by our own bootstraps" by starting in the mail room and ending up in the board room. But this healthy optimism has also led to a practical denial of the dark side of life. In religious terms, this has meant that the bad stuff has got to go — no downers, such as human depravity and inability for self-salvation, the need for divine rescue, and so forth.

Garry Wills, in his intriguing and controversial bestseller *Reagan's America*, applied James's contrasting categories to the contemporary landscape. The religion of the "sick soul" speaks of "man's fall, of the need for repentance, of humility." Wills makes this observation:

> In its Calvinistic form, this "classical" religion was important in the early history of America. But America has increasingly preferred the religion James called "healthy-mindedness," which replaces sin with sadness as the real enemy of human nature. The modern evangelicals, beaming and healthy successes in the communications industry, are exemplars of that religion.[2]

Setting aside Wills's political agenda, "feeling good" has emerged as not only a national priority but a religious obsession for Christians and non-Christians alike. It was interesting how many times during President Reagan's state funeral, reference was made to belief in the goodness of all human beings, a view that receives a nod from most evangelicals, according to some surveys.

I do not think that a biblical sense of human sin and the need for redemption outside ourselves requires national pessimism, but a religion of human goodness will never sustain a people in times of disaster and threat. We may be able to explain the "evil empires" beyond our borders by their lack of our national values. But what happens when we experience our own homegrown varieties of terrorism, violence, and social disintegration?

The religion of the healthy-minded is persuasive in our time. I think this is what Paul had in mind when he said that the Greeks were offended, bewildered, put off, by the preaching of the cross. And why not? Is Christianity supposed to be a form of masochism or passive resignation? That is clearly not the point of the message of the cross, as we will see. Yet on the surface, it has seemed compelling to many in our time that Nietzsche, Marx, and Turner are right after all, and Christianity is just a "slave morality," a way of keeping us all resigned to mediocrity and feebleness. Responding to this charge is not only an apologetic imperative, but it is essential to our own spiritual sanity.

"Glory" Is Not Enough

The irony is that the religion of Nietzsche's "superman," which the sixteenth-century Reformation dubbed a "theology of glory" in its medieval version, is its own kind of slave morality. It makes the weak subservient to the powerful, the common person to the genius, the worker to the entrepreneur, and all of this is easily supported by a church that depends on the marketplace for its own power-stake in popular culture.

Again, this is not to advocate pessimism. Because of God's common grace, even a fallen world can experience amazing tributes to justice, civic virtue, and artistic beauty. However, a religion of healthy-mindedness, which ignores the reality of the fall in all its aspects, renders itself finally nothing more than a form of therapy during times of plenty, and irrelevant in times of tragedy. What we need is not therapy, but news — good news, the kind of news that *lifts up* the downcast, *binds up* the broken, *saves* the lost, and *brings hope* to those who are at the end of their rope.

The bottom line of this book is that the gospel is good news for losers, that in fact we are all losers if we measure ourselves by God's interpretation of reality rather than our own. The demand for glory, power, comfort, autonomy, health, and wealth creates a vicious cycle of craving and disillusionment. It even creates its own industry of therapists and exercise, style, and self-esteem gurus — and churches — to massage the egos wounded by this hedonism. When crisis hits, the soul is too effete to respond appropriately. We become prisoners of our own felt needs, which were inculcated in us in the first place by the very marketplace that promises a "fix." We become victims of our own shallow hopes. We are too easily disappointed because we are too easily persuaded that the marketplace always has something that can make us happy.

As C. S. Lewis pointed out, it is not that our desires are too strong (as Stoicism would have it), but that they are too weak.[3] The irony of our lives is that we demand the ephemeral, momentary glories of this fading age, too easily amused and seduced by the trivial, when ultimate joy is held out to us.

Think of the most that we can attain in this life. Someone asked John D. Rockefeller how much money it takes to be happy, and he replied, "A little more." Consider the fame of the great stars of stage and screen whose lives we secretly wanted to share, who are now in Hollywood nursing homes, often with only memories to comfort them. How quickly adoring fans lose their interest when the vigor of youth can no longer be sustained by surgeries and lotions. No less than the rest of us, the great ones of the earth live with one foot in the grave, one payment away from repossession, one step from the abyss.

It is not pessimism, but sanity, that recognizes the truth in God's appraisal: "A voice says, 'Cry!' And I said, 'What shall I cry?' All flesh is grass, and all its beauty is like the flower of the field. The grass withers, the flower fades when the breath of the LORD blows on it; surely the people are grass. The grass withers, the flower fades, but the word of our God will stand forever" (Isaiah 40:6–8).

Again, this is not resignation to a mediocre life, but the realization that it is a life of pursuing immediate gratification, with no greater purpose or meaning, that is truly mediocre, however "high and lifted up" it may be for the moment. While life in abundance is offered to us, we settle instead for the false promises of this passing age. This "theology of glory" is hardly a recipe for fulfillment and power. Rather, it spins weakness as strength, feebleness as power, pride as humility.

What the Protestant Reformers declared in contrast to theologies of glory was the theology of the cross. In this they were simply retrieving the emphasis of the prophets, Jesus, and Paul. Ironically, it is precisely where the world detects the most obvious example of weakness — the cross — that God triumphs over sin and death at the peak of their most deadly power. Here's the irony: Just where the highest and holiest victim of truly undeserved suffering cries out, "My God, my God, why have you abandoned me?" victory over sin and death is taking place. This is the foolishness and weakness that trump the wisdom and power of the ages!

Nietzsche may have been accurately describing the feeble pietism that surrounded him, the saccharine portraits of Jesus from childhood, but he could not have been more incorrect in his analysis that as a religion of the "sick soul," the preaching of Christ was simply a message of resignation to the powers and principalities. On the contrary, it was the most radical renunciation of the herd mentality that keeps us addicted to the power brokers of this age. Of his own life, Jesus said, "No one takes it from me, but I lay it down of my own accord. I have authority to lay it down and authority to take it up again" (John 10:18 NIV). This is hardly the statement of a helpless victim. There is no sentimentalism here. No one is meant to feel sorry for Jesus. He *makes himself* a sacrificial victim, laying down his life for the sheep. Nietzsche, like we do, eventually succumbed to death. But Jesus handed himself over to it for our sakes.

In Nietzsche's view (and presumably Ted Turner's), one starts from nothing and makes something of himself. It's the rags-to-riches story. But the gospel is a different account of reality: It moves from riches to rags. The one who already had everything voluntarily, freely, without any obligation or external constraint, gave it up in order to live for others. There is a power here that makes the fallen "will to power" petty and trivial by comparison. From the moment of his acceptance of the Father's electing decree, the Son actively pursued the weakness of the incarnation, suffering, shame, and death on the cross. He fell on his own sword of justice, not as a heroic demonstration of power, but as a humble acceptance of the just sentence *we* deserved.

Strong Enough to Die

Our feeble sentimentalism simply cannot handle the tragic side of life: discomfort, sickness, disabilities, death, evil, depression, fear, anxiety. They are not realities to be faced, we tell ourselves, but symptoms of an ignored disease that we can treat with the proper medication, entertainment, therapy, and technology. "When the going gets tough, the tough go shopping." Unlike the psalmist himself, we cannot sing the laments. Even when they use the psalms, our contemporary praise choruses pick out the upbeat notes but don't know what to do with that blue note. Imagine singing one of these psalms in church next Sunday:

> *My soul refuses to be comforted.*
> *When I remember God, I moan;*
> *   when I meditate, my spirit faints.*
> *You hold my eyelids open;*
> *   I am so troubled that I cannot speak.*
> *I consider the days of old,*
> *   the years long ago. . . .*
> *"Will the Lord spurn forever,*
> *   and never again be favorable?*
> *Has his steadfast love forever ceased?*
> *   Are his promises at an end for all time?*
> *Has God forgotten to be gracious?*
> *   Has he in anger shut up his compassion?"*

Psalm 77:2 – 5, 7 – 9

For my soul is full of troubles,
and my life draws near to Sheol.
I am counted among those who go down to the pit;
I am a man who has no strength,
like one set loose among the dead,
like the slain that lie in the grave,
like those whom you remember no more,
for they are cut off from your hand.
You have put me in the depths of the pit,
in the regions dark and deep.
Your wrath lies heavy upon me,
and you overwhelm me with all your waves. . . .
You have caused my beloved and my friend to shun me;
my companions have become darkness.

Psalm 88:3–7, 18

Lord, where is your steadfast love of old,
which by your faithfulness you swore to David?

Psalm 89:49

To be sure, there are also answers to these laments: God is gracious and compassionate, faithful to his promises. Yet there is a real trial going on here, not only a trial of the human partner but of the Covenant Lord himself. Only if we allow ourselves to take seriously the empirical evidence that seems to count against God's faithfulness to his promises are we able to receive an answer that is as deep and provocative as the question.

But in contemporary piety and worship, discordant keys are not allowed; just keep it happy. Our public worship today is a fatal index of the fact that we do not know what to do in the presence of a God who is not only our friend but also our judge. We do not know what to do with sin, evil, and death in this culture, but by suppressing the question we deprive people of the comfort that comes from the answer.

This is virtually conceded by many contemporary church-growth experts. Says one, in fact, there has been a shift from "worship" to "celebrations": "The best illustration of this is that we used to have 'funerals.' Then we went to 'memorial services.' Now we have a 'celebration' of the life and ministry of the departed person. That is a shift in the whole atmosphere of what happens during that period of time. It's gone from pain, sorrow, grief, and crying, to celebration."[4] The writer regarded this as a mark of progress rather than as a sign that we are living in denial.

This response to death has been characteristic of some Eastern religions and of the ancient Gnostics who longed for the spirit's escape from the "prison-house" of the body. Such "memorials" or, indeed, "celebrations" were held by Unitarians and have been prominent in various mind-science groups, such as the Church of Scientology and Christian Science. But Judaism and Christianity have held to a somber view of death: The world was not meant to be this way. Something is wrong.

Here again we discover the contradiction in Nietzsche's "will to power." Instead of courageously facing the future, he and his followers simply deny death—at least as a real enemy. Only biblical faith faces death as a foe and, without hiding the scandal in soft platitudes, announces its conquest with military fanfare. Anchored in the Scriptures, Christians have a healthy respect for the enemy. Death is not an abstract concept but a personified character in the drama of redemption. It is death's victory, not its reality, which is overcome in Christ's resurrection.

Contrast the upbeat contemporary perspective with that of theologian Karl Barth, who was a prominent figure in the church's resistance to Nazism (one of the offspring of Nietzsche's philosophy). Each Sunday, notes Barth, the church bell is rung to announce to the village that God's word is to be proclaimed: "And if none of these things help, will not the crosses in the churchyard which quietly look in through the windows tell you unambiguously what is relevant here and what is not?"[5] The sanctuary did not see the world through rose-colored windows but through clear glass that brought reality home.

But that was when we had graveyards on church grounds. Today, we have conveniently removed death, and with it the communion of the saints, and relegated it to nondescript secular cemeteries with euphemistic names like "Forest Lawn." The average person today is about as likely to come in contact with the dead and dying as with the sources of daily bread. We now have supermarkets for everything, with cheerful music soothing any inconvenient questions, doubts, or fears about how we are dealing with life and death. Even our churches can exhibit this tendency.

In Jewish, Catholic, Reformed, Anglican, and Lutheran service books, there are specific public prayers offered for the sick and afflicted, not a general, one-size-fits-all response. There are prayers for wartime, natural disasters, epidemics, a sick child, those in bereavement, travelers, and prisoners. In Puritan families, the body of the deceased was normally placed in an open casket in a central living space until the funeral itself. Children could ask about its meaning. Ministers visiting those on their deathbed would ask them directly, "Are you prepared to die?" Some wrote eloquently and wisely on the art of dying well. But this is not likely to become part of the "reality TV" fare in our day.

To be sure, a lot of this has to do with historical circumstances. Whenever a people seem outwardly prosperous, they are less prepared to spend time thinking about tragedy, while times of great suffering can get people thinking a lot about something other than the season finale of their favorite TV show or the big game. That which Paul says about individual believers can be said also more corporately:

Therefore, since we have been justified by faith, we have peace with God through our Lord Jesus Christ. Through him we have also obtained access by faith into this grace in which we stand, and we rejoice in hope of the glory of God. More than that, we rejoice in our sufferings, knowing that suffering produces endurance, and endurance produces character, and character produces hope, and hope does not put us to shame, because God's love has been poured into our hearts through the Holy Spirit who has been given to us. For while we were still weak, at the right time Christ died for the ungodly.

Romans 5:1–6

During the mid-seventeenth century, as many as one-third of London's population died, either in the plague or in the great fire. In New England, things were not much better for London's Puritan contemporaries, given the harsh conditions, each winter leaving death in its wake. People did not have the time to complain about their treatment at work or their dysfunctional parents. It was not because they were stoics, but because they were veterans of sickness, suffering, and death. They learned that they had to either reach more deeply into God's Word for sustenance or simply follow the advice of Job's wife: "Curse God and die!"

The Book of Common Prayer has a service for the burial of the dead—not the burial of the deceased, or the resting, or those who have, in the now widely adopted parlance of Christian Science founder Mary Baker Eddy, "passed on," but the *dead*. It begins with the glorious promise of future resurrection. But then the Book of Common Prayer cites the psalmist:

Lord, let me know mine end, and the number of my days; that I may be certified how long I have to live. Behold, thou hast made my days as it were a span long, and mine age is even as nothing in respect of thee; and verily every man living is altogether vanity. For man walketh in a vain shadow, and disquieteth himself in vain; he heapeth up riches, and cannot tell who shall gather them. And now, LORD, what is my hope? truly my hope is even in thee.... When thou with rebukes dost chasten man for sin, thou makest his beauty to waste away, like as it were a moth fretting a garment: every man therefore is but vanity. Hear my prayer, O LORD, and with thine ears consider my cry; hold not thy peace at my tears: For I am a stranger with thee, and a sojourner, as all my fathers were. O spare me a little, that I may recover my strength, before I go hence, and be no more seen (Psalm 39).

Passages of hope are then recited from the Psalms, Gospels, and Epistles, affirming the resurrection of the body and the free justification of all who trust in Christ. Then comes the sober prayer:

O God, whose days are without end, and whose mercies cannot be numbered; make us, we beseech thee, deeply sensible of the shortness and uncertainty of human life; and let thy Holy Spirit lead us through this vale of misery, in holiness and righteousness, all the days of our lives: That, when we shall have served thee in our generation, we may be gathered unto our fathers, having the testimony of a good conscience; in the communion of thy church; in the confidence of a certain faith; in the comfort of a reasonable, religious, and holy hope; in favor with thee our God, and in perfect charity with the world. All which we ask through Jesus Christ our Lord. Amen.

Shaped by the psalms, this prayer anchors our hope in God and his purposes for our lives instead of in us and ours. The goal of life is not to be happy, but to be holy; not to make ourselves acceptable to ourselves and others, but to be made acceptable *to* God *by* God; not to be gathered together with all of the successful people in the prime of our life, but to be gathered unto our fathers and mothers in the faith. There is no place for suffering in a life whose goals are determined by a hedonistic culture, but if our chief end is "to glorify God and to enjoy him forever," as the Westminster Shorter Catechism has it, and our lives are read in light of the broader script of creation, fall, and redemption, then suffering is the way to ultimate glory, not a resignation to meaningless tragedy.

chapter three
suffering on purpose

Neither this chapter nor this book aims to address the larger theoretical problem of evil. In fact, I do not believe there is a satisfying *theoretical* answer for us in this life. But, better than that, there is a *practical* answer. It is the cross and resurrection.

Instead of trying to solve the mystery of evil, I want to relate a specific biblical theme to the practical situation of those who suffer and grieve. In the cross and resurrection, God does not *explain* the problem of evil to our satisfaction but actually *overcomes* it in a way that surprises and overwhelms us. It may not be good philosophy, but it's great theater — and the stage is actual human history, where certain revolutionary events have *happened*, not abstract speculation about *the way things "are."*

I have been amazed in recent years to see just how central is the contrast between the theology of glory and the theology of the cross in the Gospels. This contrast was brought out with great clarity in the Protestant Reformation, by Martin Luther especially, but also by John Calvin and other Reformers. After all, the context of their lives was suffering on a broad, as well as on a personal, scale. The infamous Plague ("Black Death") had claimed about a third of Europe's population in the mid-1300s. Wars and poverty were still rampant. Calvin suffered from a host of crippling ailments throughout his adult life, mourned the death of his own child, and received daily reports about the gruesome martyrdoms of his fellow Frenchmen, which deeply grieved him. Doubtless, these experiences brought urgency to the demand for robust answers to their anxieties about the future. They turned with fresh appreciation to the biblical preaching of the cross.

Basically summarized, their point amounts to this: The theology of glory sees God everywhere, in glory and in power, and presumes to ascend self-confidently to God by means of experience, rational speculation, and merit. It is the religion of the natural man or woman. By contrast, the theology of the cross sees God only where God has revealed himself, particularly in the weakness and mercy of the suffering. Only when we learn to despair of ourselves, to suffer our own nakedness in God's holy presence, to renounce our righteousness and listen only to God's Word, are we enabled to recognize God as our Savior rather than our just judge and holy enemy. We rise up to God in pride, while God descends to us in humility. We look for God in powerful places; in health, wealth, and happiness; in perfect families and prosperous nations, but God is truly to be found in the weak things of the world. In other words, we are talking about a theology for winners versus a theology for losers.

This theme is central to Paul's teaching, for example, in 1 Corinthians:

> For the word of the cross is folly to those who are perishing, but to us who are being saved it is the power of God. For it is written,

> "I will destroy the wisdom of the wise,
>   and the discernment of the discerning I will thwart."

> Where is the one who is wise? Where is the scribe? Where is the debater of this age? Has not God made foolish the wisdom of the world? For since, in the wisdom of God,

*the world did not know God through wisdom, it pleased
God through the folly of what we preach to save those who
believe. For Jews demand signs and Greeks seek wisdom,
but we preach Christ crucified, a stumbling block to Jews
and folly to Gentiles, but to those who are called, both
Jews and Greeks, Christ the power of God and the wisdom of God. For the foolishness of God is wiser than men,
and the weakness of God is stronger than men.*

*For consider your calling, brothers: not many of you
were wise according to worldly standards, not many were
powerful, not many were of noble birth. But God chose what
is foolish in the world to shame the wise; God chose what is
weak in the world to shame the strong; God chose what is low
and despised in the world, even things that are not, to bring
to nothing things that are, so that no human being might
boast in the presence of God.*

1 Corinthians 1:18–29

In our Redeemer's years on earth, the God who had created heaven and earth was now incarnate. He started out dependent on a poor couple barely capable of providing for their
own basic needs. As Jesus approached his messianic vocation,
John the Baptist announced, "Behold, the Lamb of God, who
takes away the sin of the world!" (John 1:29). So from the very
beginning, Jesus lived under the shadow of the cross. It was
not only on Good Friday, but from the moment he assumed
our flesh and endured our shame, that he began to suffer for
our redemption. He was recognized by the Old Testament and
identified by John as the substitutionary sacrifice.

As John baptized him, Jesus knew exactly what would happen. This baptism not only fulfilled all righteousness, but it
also consecrated Jesus as Lamb of God. In other words, it sealed
his death already. The heavenly voice responded, "This is my

beloved Son, with whom I am well pleased" (Matthew 3:17; 17:5). So we already see the paradox emerging: The Father expresses his greatest pleasure in his Son precisely at those moments when the storm clouds of Good Friday gather on the horizon. The crucifixion is not something that happens to Jesus on his way to doing something else, like showing us how "good guys finish first," or how to make a difference in the world, or how to be a successful leader.

It was in these moments of greatest humiliation for the Son that God is most pleased, not because God likes to see people suffer, much less his only begotten Son. It's no morbid interest on God's part; God's joy lies in the result:

> *Yet it was the will of the LORD to crush him with pain.*
> *When you make his life an offering for sin,*
> *   he shall see his offspring, and shall prolong his days;*
> *through him the will of the LORD shall prosper.*
> *   Out of his anguish he shall see light;*
> *he shall find satisfaction through his knowledge.*
> *   The righteous one, my servant, shall make many righteous,*
> *   and he shall bear their iniquities.*

Isaiah 53:10–11 NRSV

A *Good* Crucifixion?

If we ever question — and if you haven't yet, you will — the reliability of that famous assurance that "for those who love God all things work together for good, for those who are called according to his purpose" (Romans 8:28), we have before us a dilemma. How could the incarnation, suffering, humiliation, and eventual death of the Son of God be explained in anything but tragic terms? Who among us was *least* deserving of his lot in life? And yet, unlike most instances of our suffering in the world, in this case we know not only *that*, but *how* and *why* all things worked together for our good in those events.

All along the way, there were obstacles. The first, not surprisingly, came from Lucifer, the first theologian of glory, who had led the first Adam astray and had no doubt tempted Israel to demand food in the wilderness instead of trusting in every word that comes from the mouth of God. Now he sought to draw the second Adam into satisfying his own felt needs by choosing worldly pomp ("the kingdoms of the world") over the cross. Taking Satan's route, Jesus could secure power, money, success, and happiness right here, right now. Total security. Never wondering whether there was enough in the bank account to cover an expense, he would have the world at his feet. No more dusty days and homeless nights, enduring the humiliation of insults and unbelief from the very people who had been prepared by the prophets to welcome him. Glory for himself now, instead of the cross — that was the temptation (Matthew 4:1 – 11).

If it were only Satan's temptation, we could understand it. After all, he is "the father of lies" (John 8:44). But even the disciples seemed to misunderstand their master's teaching. Repeatedly throughout the Gospels, Jesus was on a clear road leading from Galilee to Jerusalem. There was no press conference in Galilee to boost his career. In fact, his early ministry was marked by secrecy about his identity, which is one of the reasons he was somewhat disturbed by his mother's insistence that he replenish the wine supply at the wedding reception (John 2:1 – 12).

But as Jesus went along that road toward Jerusalem, more signs accompanied increasingly clear announcements about this person and work. Crowds began pressing on him and his disciples. He tried to confide in his disciples, explaining what this mission was all about, but they kept changing the subject every time he brought up his impending death. Even for Jesus' own brothers, who did not yet believe in him, Jesus was a marketable product (John 7:3–4). It was the theology of glory, the religion of the "healthy-minded" type: optimistic, revolutionary, victorious. The disciples saw Jerusalem as the big time, the payoff for all their labors: "If I can make it there, I'll make it anywhere," as Sinatra sang about New York City. "We're going to Jerusalem all right," Jesus kept saying, "but it will be nothing like what you have in mind."

Mark's gospel especially underscores the repeated times that Jesus tried to explain his death and resurrection. Finally, Peter, weary of all this talk about the theology of the cross, rebuked his Master:

> *Then [Jesus] began to teach them that the Son of Man must undergo great suffering, and be rejected by the elders, the chief priests, and the scribes, and be killed, and after three days rise again. He said all this quite openly. And Peter took him aside and began to rebuke him. But turning and looking at his disciples, he rebuked Peter and said, "Get behind me, Satan! For you are setting your mind not on divine things but on human things."*

Mark 8:31–33 NRSV

"Divine things" here corresponds to God's plan of redemption through the cross; "human things" corresponds to the theology of glory. Like the Pharisees, the disciples were often more impressed with Jesus' signs-and-wonders ministry than with his words to which the signs pointed. So from this rebuke Jesus launched into a sermon:

> *He called the crowd with his disciples, and said to them, "If any want to become my followers, let them deny themselves and take up their cross and follow me. For those who want to save their life will lose it, and those who lose their life for my sake, and for the sake of the gospel,*

*will save it. For what will it profit them to gain the whole
world and forfeit their life?"*

Mark 8:34–36 NRSV

Jesus would come with power, to liberate and to judge, in
great splendor and majesty, as the disciples were anticipating when
they rolled into Jerusalem. But that was not to be the purpose of
this trip, Jesus said (Mark 9:1). They had confused Christ's first
coming in weakness with his second coming in power.

On an earlier occasion James and John had wanted to call
down fire on a Samaritan village that refused to hear the gospel, but "Jesus turned and rebuked them, and they went to another village" (Luke 9:55–56 NIV).

In Mark 10, Jesus explained his impending death and resurrection once again. And what was the disciples' response this
time? James and John put in a petition for their rank in the
kingdom of glory: "Grant us to sit, one at your right hand and
one at your left, in your glory" (Mark 10:37). Did they hear
anything about the cross? Did they get *any* of it? Jerusalem, for
the disciples, still meant Jesus' coronation day in the capital,
and they could barely sleep at night, picturing themselves on
the platform with him.

But here was Jesus' response to this fresh effusion of the
theology of glory: "'You do not know what you are asking. Are
you able to drink the cup that I drink, or be baptized with
the baptism that I am baptized with?' They replied, 'We are
able'" (Mark 10:38–39 NRSV). What audacity! They were
thinking he would be anointed king. What they were hearing
was this: *Can you bear the awesome burden, as well as dignity,
of being consecrated along with me?* But what Jesus was actually saying—and had been saying often—was that the coming
baptism was death! And no ordinary death. It was going to
be the cruelest, most despicable form of execution, reserved for

the greatest capital offenses — and furthermore, it would be the judicial curse of his Father, cutting him off from the land of the living. In fact, his disciples' fear for their own lives would leave him bereft of all comfort, alone in a hell of splinters and nails, with all of heaven's wrath weighing down on his brow.

This is why Jesus answered James and John, "You do not know what you are asking." Mercifully, the brothers' request was not answered. They were not crowned on Jesus' right and left hand that day on Golgotha. They did not endure divine condemnation. Jesus went to his dreaded throne alone, for them. Jesus gathers the disciples close to him to indicate the kind of kingdom he is inaugurating, so contrary to their apparent expectations:

> *You know that among the Gentiles those whom they recognize as their rulers lord it over them, and their great ones are tyrants over them. But it is not so among you; but whoever wishes to become great among you must be your servant, and whoever wishes to be first among you must be slave of all. For the Son of Man came not to be served but to serve, and to give his life a ransom for many.*

> Mark 10:42–45 NRSV

Gentile power brokers put their enemies on crosses in order to get to the top; this ruler puts *himself* on one *for* his enemies.

Whenever Jesus brought up his death with the disciples, they either rebuked him for morbidity or changed the subject to a more uplifting, upbeat, edifying topic. Like all of us, they wanted the healthy-minded religion, not the religion of the sick soul. But the Father and the Holy Spirit responded differently. When Jesus willingly embraced the cross in his baptism, the Holy Spirit's benediction was heard.

And now, for the fourth time, Jesus spoke at length concerning his death, and again the Father and the Holy Spirit testified to the Son's ministry. In fact, the only times in the Gospels where we read of a voice coming from heaven are when Jesus obediently embraced the cross:

> *"Now my soul is troubled. And what should I say— 'Father, save me from this hour'? No, it is for this reason that I have come to this hour. Father, glorify your name." Then a voice came from heaven, "I have glorified it, and I will glorify it again." The crowd standing there heard it and said that it was thunder. Others said, "An angel has spoken to him." Jesus answered, "This voice has come for your sake, not for mine. Now is the judgment of this world; now the ruler of this world will be driven out. And I, when I am lifted up from the earth, will draw all people to myself." He said this to indicate the kind of death he was to die.*

John 12:27–33 NRSV

What is so remarkable is that as the disciples fled the crucifixion scene, it was a Roman military officer who, amid the clamor of thunder and under the shroud of darkness, declared, "Truly this man was the Son of God!" (Mark 15:39). Only after the resurrection did Jesus find his dejected disciples and explain to them how everything that had just occurred was according to plan—and not only God's secret plan by which he works all things together for good, but according to his unfolding plan in history, which was largely available to them if they would only have read the Scriptures, with Christ and the gospel at the center.

Like the Pharisees, who had closely studied the Bible without the key piece of the puzzle (namely, Christ himself, John 5:39), those who were most expecting glory on Palm Sunday were bitterly crying, "Crucify him!" on Good Friday, while many of the disciples themselves scattered. They did not understand any of it until Easter morning. Despite the message of the cross running from Genesis 3 to Malachi 4, they simply did not have the theological coordinates for this unfolding plot. Consequently, their triumphalism turned to despair. That's how the risen Christ found them (see Luke 24:13–35).

So where is God amid so much suffering? Hanging on the cross, bearing in his own body the curse of his own law, drinking the cup of wrath and the venom of our sin and death. Even though we cannot see God's sovereignty and goodness reconciled in holocausts, tsunamis, hurricanes, and fires, here the harmony is empirically verifiable! God is neither aloof to our suffering nor powerless to intervene.

No one has ever suffered more unjustly at our hands than this sinless God-Man, and yet he was "delivered up according to the definite plan and foreknowledge of God" (Acts 2:23). We can be assured that in the crises we face, large and small, God works all things together for good (see Romans 8:28) because God's strength has once and for all been made perfect in weakness. The unity of God's sovereignty and goodness that will be fully disclosed on the last day has already dawned decisively in the work of Christ. God has triumphed over the serpent, sin, death, evil, and tragedy. "It is finished!" Jesus cried. Our victory is assured, though we walk through the valley of death's shadow (Psalm 23:4). In fact, in this famous psalm of comfort in distress, we can say, "I will fear no evil, for you are with me; your rod and your staff, they comfort me."

The shepherd imagery in Scripture is not simply what we associate with animal husbandry. In the ancient Near East, "shepherd" was royal language. The king protected his subjects at the cost of his own life. His rod and staff were equivalent to the scepter and mace held by monarchs on their throne. In Christ — that is, under his guardianship — we are assured that God, not Satan, is king; life, not death, has the last word; righteousness, not sin, reigns over us; blessing, not condemnation, is our inheritance here and now. "The sting of death is sin, and the power of sin is the law. But thanks be to God, who gives us the victory through our Lord Jesus Christ" (1 Corinthians 15:56–57).

Taking Up Our Cross

Renowned pastor and mentor James Montgomery Boice, in his final address to his congregation in center-city Philadelphia not long before he succumbed to pancreatic cancer in 2000, said, "I am not asking that you pray for my recovery, but that in my death I will bring glory to my faithful Savior." I told him I would pray for his recovery anyway, and he didn't seem to mind, but his point was that as horrible as our own circumstances may be, they are secondary to our salvation and God's glory.

When I read those words posted on the Internet, I thought of a sermon on Jonah I had heard Jim preach. "God's grace is not a way of going *around* trials," he declared, "but a way of going *through* them." It is true, of course. God nowhere promises us temporal prosperity, but the way he has redeemed us makes all of our trials cruciform, that is, shaped not by the circumstances themselves but by the suffering and victory of Christ.

Scripture treats our sharing in Christ's sufferings as the prerequisite for our sharing in his glory (Romans 8:17; 2 Corinthians 1:5; Philippians 1:29; 1 Peter 4:13). First and foremost, the cross is *Christ's* cross, which, as we have seen, no one else is able to bear. That cross alone brings forgiveness of sins and peace with God. His suffering was redemptive, whereas ours is a participation in that already-accomplished victory. But our cross bearing is still real. It is not another cross that we bear, our own burden for sin and guilt, but sharing in his humiliation and shame as those who belong to him. Most central in Paul's discussion of this matter is suffering for the name of Christ — in other words, the kind of trials associated with persecution. However, Paul himself broadens it to include all manner of suffering (Romans 5:3 – 4).

So it is not by imitating Christ's vicarious and atoning death, but by being incorporated into it as members organically attached to their dying and living Head, that his conquest of sin and death becomes ours. The gospel, then, is not an appeal to resign ourselves to the powers and principalities, as Nietzsche and his heirs would assert. Rather, it is the invitation to surrender our life voluntarily under the reign of sin and death, in order to get it back again as part of God's new creation.

This is what Jesus meant when he said, "Whoever finds his life will lose it, and whoever loses his life for my sake will find it" (Matthew 10:39). A seed is sown in weakness, said Paul, but is raised from its wintry night to yield abundant fruit (see 1 Corinthians 15:42 – 49). The message we are given to proclaim is not that God has come to make our lives better, more interesting, more influential, more virtuous, or more successful, but to bury us and make us truly alive.

In my personal and pastoral experience, I have noticed that those who demand heaven on earth here and now — instant health, wealth, happiness, or holiness — often become the most embittered, hostile, and disillusioned critics of Christianity. Whether it is perfect bodies, perfect sanctification, perfect success, perfect marriages, perfect children, perfect security, perfect churches — whatever — we must abandon this theology of glory instead of abandoning the God who works all things together for good.

Notice that God *works all things* together for our good. This does not mean we are to call everything that happens to us "good." The terrible things that happen to us and to our loved ones rightly fill us with grief, sap our strength, and trouble our souls. Sickness and death, suffering and pain, remain matters to be taken with the appropriate seriousness, not to be trivialized on the one hand, or sentimentalized or celebrated on the other. It is true that we do not mourn as those who have no hope (1 Thessalonians 4:13), but we *do* mourn. There is both a time to laugh and a time to mourn (Ecclesiastes 3). What we believe about God and his revealed purposes in history — in other words, our theology — shapes how we experience both in proper proportion. The book of Psalms includes the full range of human emotion because it includes the full range of biblical theology. We need to recapture the theological and emotional maturity of this inspired hymnal, refusing to settle for happy jingles and exultant anthems that exclude the blues.

As for ourselves, we must take up our cross, neither avoiding it nor seeking it. As Luther said, the cross finds us. This is no call to a "martyr's complex" that acquiesces to suffering, evil, sin, or pain for ourselves or others — still less, to pretend that the cross of splinters is really a cause for celebration instead of mourning. But it is to be prepared to "let goods and kindred go, this mortal life also," for the sake of the kingdom whose treasures far outweigh and outlast anything we can know in this fading age.

Beyond Chicken Soup

Christianity *is* for the weak and oppressed. On that score, Nietzsche and his disciples were correct. They will tell us that our "explanation" of the problem of evil is philosophically inadequate. And of course it is — especially to those who will not accept God's interpretation of reality. The philosophers will talk about reconciling a certain notion of God with a certain notion of freedom and then taking evil into account and attempt a final resolution. But the gospel will tell a story about a good God who created and rules over all, bringing salvation out of the misery we have brought on ourselves.

But even then, we can talk about the creation of the world and of humanity in righteousness, original sin, the curse on all aspects of life because of the fall, and God's provision of redemption from the curse in Jesus Christ. We can speak with great hope of the age to come when our bodies will be raised — an event for which the whole natural world groans, since it, too, will share in the glorious liberty of God's children (Romans 8).

But at the end of the day, suffering is still an enigma, even to us. Yet it is only a problem because something in us knows that this is not the way it was meant to be, that there is something more, that there is a purpose for everything in the future.

Nietzsche and his disciples may have correctly identified that Christianity is for the weak and not for self-confident individuals in their will to power. But because he who was rich for our sakes became poor, he who was powerful for our sakes became weak, and he who was wise for our sakes became foolish, the meek "shall inherit the earth" in him (Matthew 5:5). To healthy-minded optimists, Jesus announces that he has come for the sick, not for the healthy. We need something more than chicken soup for our souls; we need to be transferred from the domain of sin and death into the kingdom of God's Son. We need hope, and not the kind of hope expressed in the American Dream or in the vague sentimentalism of Jiminy Cricket's "wishing upon a star," but rather "a sure and steadfast anchor of the soul, a hope that enters into the inner place behind the curtain, where Jesus has gone as a forerunner on our behalf, having become a high priest forever after the order of Melchizedek" (Hebrews 6:19 – 20).

While some professing Christians have perpetrated enormous injustices in the name of Christianity throughout the ages, more people have died under the experimental reign of Nietzsche and his disciples (most notably, Hitler and Stalin) than in all of the previous centuries combined. The full-strength theology of glory embraced by Nietzsche and his nihilistic disciples in our own time represents a power that would crush all weakness. But the theology of the cross proclaimed, embraced, and enacted by the Suffering Servant has stripped from the powers of darkness their ultimate threat and will in due season trample all enemies underfoot.

The good news announced so long ago, sealed by the Suffering Servant and his victory over sin and death, is still held out to those who are weary of being "supermen," are tired of being cynical, and who are ready to exchange their theology of glory for a theology of the cross: "Come to me, all of you who are weary and weighted down, and I will give you rest" (Matthew 11:28, my translation).

chapter four
is your GOD big enough?

William James, father of America's homegrown philosophy known as pragmatism (that is, truth is whatever works best for the greatest number of people), said that the test of a religious claim is "its cash-value in experiential terms." "On pragmatistic principles, if the hypothesis of God works satisfactorily in the widest sense of the word, it is true." Religion, on this conception, is "merely melioristic [therapeutic] in type." "God is not worshiped," said James, "he is used." We choose our religion, or leave it behind, based on whether we perceive its relevance for making our lives better. In short, we believe because it works, not because it's "true."[1]

A recent study by leading sociologist Christian Smith confirms that America's teens are not antireligious, but rather seem fairly committed to what Smith characterizes as "moralistic, therapeutic deism."[2] In a similar analysis of sermons in evangelical and mainline churches, Marsha G. Witten, a self-described non-Christian sociologist, concluded much the same, showing that the content of preaching differs little between evangelical and more "liberal" churches.[3]

The assumption, of course, is that we never really encounter God—a person distinct from us—but only our personal, national, or cultural ideas of "god." We never experience *God*, but only our own *experiences* of God. "God" therefore amounts to "whatever we need."

We have already noted that the popular culture increasingly views God's role in our lives as merely a therapeutic enterprise. This is not a new observation, of course. Modern atheism (Feuerbach, Nietzsche, Marx, Freud) has consistently argued that "god" is no more than a psychological projection of one's own needs for transcendent comfort in the face of overwhelming pressures. Only weak people need "god," and religion continually reinforces their reticence to take life into their own hands. This objection (raised in the previous chapter) relates to our concept of God. Is God just a projection of our own felt needs? Do we just adopt conceptions that fit with our experience, that reinforce our preconceived ideas and expectations?

Of course, truth isn't like that. We know that we have drilled into reality when its gushing intensity throws us off balance. But to come into contact with your own psychic projections is simply to reinforce existing assumptions rather than to be acted upon by something external. What we're really talking about here is *idolatry*. After all, meeting the real God who is there, who has spoken through the prophets and apostles, culminating in his own Son, is pretty unsettling. Idols confirm what we already assume about reality; the God of Israel confuses us.

Some years ago now, J. B. Phillips wrote his splendid little classic titled *Your God Is Too Small*, in which he argued that the deity of many Christians is far too feeble to handle adolescent and adult crises. When suffering comes, many who have never gotten beyond sentimental images of God find they simply do not have a God worth trusting when the going gets tough.

In recent debates even within evangelical circles, this combination of experience-centeredness (religion as therapy) and sentimentalized pictures of God has become especially problematic. Challenging the classical Christian doctrine of God, a growing circle of evangelical theologians and pastors argues that God does not control everything that happens or, for that matter, *know* everything that will happen. Rather, "in loving dialogue, God invites us to participate with him to bring the future into being." What is desperately needed, we are told, is a theology "that reinforces, rather than makes problematic, our relational experience with God."[4] In such statements we discern the broad outlines of that fatal combination: experience-centeredness and sentimentalized pictures of God. And when tragedy strikes, the sentimentalized pictures actually become shattered fragments of a childhood faith.

Letting our experience be our guide just makes a lot of sense on the surface, doesn't it? After all, our senses are our "feelers" that simply collect data, and our experience then merely registers the facts of the case, right? Actually, this is a pretty naive view of experience—or any human faculty. As we are realizing more and more these days, our experience (no less than our thoughts) is conditioned. There are no neutral, value-free data. There are no brute facts of existence—that is, raw givens that do not have to be interpreted. Our experience is always laden already with a host of prior assumptions, some explicit and others implicit.

We are not aware of a whole variety of presuppositions that we use, even unwittingly, to interpret experience. For example, when you read the Pilgrims of the Plymouth colony describing in their own words the layers of hardship they endured, confidence in God's providence led them to interpret their trials rather differently from the way followers of the prosperity gospel today would explain their obstacles. There is no theology-free experience. It is all interpreted, and the question is whether there is something outside our experience to critique it, to let it know whether it got things right. If experience is normative—that is, the judge and jury—then modern atheism is probably right in claiming that "God" is not an objective reality outside of our own projections, but is someone we have "created"—like the imaginary friend of childhood, in order to support our currently reigning presuppositions about reality.

Following our experience means we are always prisoners of what we already believe. If we simply let our heart be our guide, we'll never be challenged, corrected, surprised, or changed in a more liberating direction. It is not so much that an atheist fails to experience reality, but that he or she experiences it *as* life without God. The interpretation (that is, theology—even for an atheist!) shapes how one experiences things, even if two people are encountering precisely the same crisis. For someone who denies that Jesus is God in the flesh coming to our rescue, what experience could count in favor of the resurrection? As Jesus himself said to the religious leaders, "You would not believe, even if God were to raise someone from the dead" (Luke 16:31, my translation).

God on His Own Terms

Ironically, it can be experience itself that calls our hand in this matter, forcing us to choose whether we will allow it to be the judge or the accused. It is actually a piece of good news that our experience does not have the last word, that even in the face of horrific evils, tragedies, temptations, and doubts, the supposedly obvious deliverances of experience can be mistaken; that God may be actually more present in saving mercies when our experience tells us he is most distant and unconcerned. This is a key point of the theology of the cross: God is most *present* precisely where he seems most *absent*. Again, this isn't a general speculation, an easy way of accepting the situation despite all evidence to the contrary; rather, it is grounded in the empirical fact of God's saving work in Christ. Both our *questioning* of God's purposes and *confidence* in them are provoked by empirical reality. The events that prove God's faithfulness occur on the same plane of history as those that challenge it. Therefore, it is the empirical events of the cross and resurrection, not of daily events whose meaning is *not* revealed to us, that demonstrate the reliability of God's character.

Although "making man the measure" of truth, specifically via experience, is most obviously identified with modern (liberal) theology, it is widely accepted, at least in practice, across the entire theological spectrum today. I am amazed by the extent to which some Christian theologians are willing to reject the traditional understanding of God for a theology "that reinforces, rather than makes problematic, our relational experience with God." Consider how whenever Jesus proclaimed the kingdom, even those who should have known better were offended and left him. Recall Paul's claim that the gospel is "foolishness to those who are perishing" (1 Corinthians 1:18 NRSV).

In fact, the whole purpose of preaching is to make alive those who are spiritually dead, to turn hearts of stone into hearts of flesh, to bring about repentance—a change of mind that recognizes just how wrong one's experience and reason has been—all of this leading to faith in Christ. We are exhorted to "no longer be conformed to this world's pattern of thinking, but [to] be transformed by the renewing of [our] mind" (Romans 12:2, my translation).

This assumes, of course, that reality is not the projection of our own heads or hearts, but exists apart from us. C. S. Lewis captures this point so well in connection with pantheism—the view that all is divine, thus confusing the Creator with his creation. "People," he says, "are reluctant to pass over from the notion of an abstract and negative deity to the living God." Lewis adds:

> I do not wonder. Here lies the deepest tap-root of Pantheism and of the objection to traditional imagery. It

was hated not, at bottom, because it pictured Him as man but because it pictured Him as king, or even as warrior. The Pantheist's God does nothing, demands nothing. He is there if you wish for Him, like a book on a shelf. He will not pursue you.... [But it] is always shocking to meet life where we thought we were alone. "Look out!" we cry, "it's alive!" And therefore this is the very point at which so many draw back—I would have done so myself if I could—and proceed no further with Christianity. An "impersonal God"—well and good. A subjective God of beauty, truth and goodness, inside our own heads—better still. A formless life-force surging through us, a vast power which we can tap—best of all. But God Himself, alive, pulling at the other end of the cord, perhaps approaching at an infinite speed, the hunter, king, husband—that is quite another matter.[5]

To be sure, those in our circles who are challenging the traditional doctrine of God are not pantheists. But given that this is the case, why do they allow human experience to determine truth? After all, if God is not only immanent (that is, up close and involved in our lives) but also transcendent (that is, above us, beyond us, different from us, glorious in power and wisdom), then *his* interpretation of reality, even of our own reality, must be the judge of our experience. We do not know God reliably from our experience (that is, *our* interpretation of reality) but from God's revelation (that is, *his* interpretation of reality). This is the basic starting point for all sound theology.

In fact, Christian theology is specifically charged with the task of *making problematic* our relationship with God, of presenting God to ourselves and others in such a way as to be confronted with a person who cannot be conformed to the narrow and, we must add, sinful precincts of our own longings, expectations, and concepts. The God who comes to us in revelation is not a projection, but a person. He wrestles us to the ground, takes away our pride, and leaves us walking away from the match with a limp so that we will never forget the encounter.

Having argued that Scripture and not our own experience should decide these matters, the next question is this: With what kind of God does Scripture confront us? It sounds easy to say that Scripture should decide the matter, but we soon realize that Scripture also is something we must interpret. How can we do so faithfully?

A recurring presupposition of this book is that we can only interpret Scripture faithfully if we read it with Christ at the center. Christ is the Living Word, God's own revelation of himself in the flesh. We can take our favorite verses from Scripture and piece them together to match our idea of God, but it is only in Christ that God's transcendence (difference and distance from us) and immanence (nearness), power and weakness, sovereignty and grace, justice and mercy, wrath and love, come to their clearest expression. From a Christian perspective, mere theism — that is, simply defending a view of God that is common to monotheists (Jews, Muslims, and Christians) — has no solution whatsoever to the problem of evil. Here it is true that "God" is the problem, not the answer. We will easily end up in either deism (God as uninvolved) or pantheism (God as indistinguishable from creation).

In Christ, however, the God who is utterly distinct from creation has nevertheless become a part of creation without losing his transcendence in the bargain. "The Word became flesh and pitched his tent among us" (John 1:14, my translation). God is in no way dependent on the world, and yet he became involved to such a degree that he willingly assumed our flesh, endured suffering at our hand, and bore our just sentence on the cross.

Let us move on then to specific challenges.

Challenges to God's Might

Most Christians down through the ages would have concluded that the recent trend to measure God by our own experience, rejecting his omnipotence and omniscience, is a direct rejection of the first article of the Apostles' Creed: "I believe in God the Father, Almighty." If God is *good*, some theologians argue, he would surely have stopped the Holocaust if he could have; therefore, he simply must not have been *able* to do so. Especially in the light of horrific historical events, but also no doubt weakened by a failure to teach an adequate view of God over generations, our age tends to opt for this horn of the dilemma. Better to have a God who would keep bad things from happening if he could than to have a God who allows or even purposes evil and suffering, it is said in such bestsellers as Rabbi Harold Kushner's *When Bad Things Happen to Good People.*

This view so identifies God with the world that the Creator and his creation are nearly fused. But pantheism and atheism are not that far apart. (In fact, in Buddhism, they are one and the same.) After all, if everything is in some sense divine, then there is really no place for a distinctly personal God. In the 1960s, the "Death of God" theologians argued this so forcefully that *Time* magazine gave them a cover story—a black field with bold red letters, "Is God Dead?"

Others have been more restrained: God is not dead, but he is suffering. He is a victim along with the rest of us. He would like to turn things around for us, but he cannot, or will not, because of the higher value he places on our freedom.

Although hardly a conservative theologian himself, Hans Küng offers a sound critique of this position, as it is inspired more by Hegel (a nineteenth-century German philosopher) than by the Bible. Küng has spent much of his life interacting with the Holocaust as a Swiss Catholic theologian (and a renegade to boot). Yet he correctly observes that we cannot do away with the "goodness" of God in order to find an easy explanation of suffering. He writes:

> A look at Scripture may sober up such speculative boldness. Granted, in anthropomorphic language the Hebrew Bible sometimes attributes the whole range of human feelings and attitudes to God. But nowhere is the difference between God and human beings done away with, nor is human suffering and pain simply declared to be the suffering and pain of God. Nowhere does God's Godliness become ungodliness, his faithfulness unfaithfulness, his reliability unreliability, his divine mercy human pitifulness. For the Hebrew Bible, though human beings fail, God does not fail; when human beings die, God does not die also. For "I am God and not man, the holy one in your midst," states Hosea 11:9 against any humanization of God, although at this very point as elsewhere there is anthropomorphic talk of God's "compassion" on his people.[6]

Concerning God's unchanging character, the New Testament tells the same story. Jesus cries out to his Father, "My God, my God, why have you forsaken me?" (Matthew 27:46) not because God suffers just as we do but because the Son was made "in all points like us, yet without sin" (Hebrews 4:15, my translation). Küng encourages us to "emphatically protest against a masochistic, tolerant understanding of God according to which a weak God has to torture himself to resurrection by suffering and death if he is not to suffer eternally."[7]

Centuries of believers have correctly concluded from reading the Scriptures that God is in charge. First, God is self-sufficient. Alone the source of life, he is dependent on no one and no thing for his existence or happiness. This means that when God does enter into relationships with his creatures, it is entirely free and spontaneous. Unlike the gods of Greek mythology, the true God is not "served by human hands, as though he needed anything, since he himself gives to all mankind life and breath and everything" (Acts 17:25). God did not create us because he was lonely or bored, but because he was so full of vitality and an overabundance of joy that he freely willed to share himself! He didn't have to create us, but he did. We are the result of God's liberal freedom and love, not of his neediness and lack.

Second, God is unchangeable in his nature and purposes. While God's *revealed* designs are often made contingent on the actions of his covenant partners, God's *secret* plans are already settled, long before we arrived on the scene. The psalmist notes that while God changes the ancient heavens and the earth as a nurse changes diapers, he himself does not change: "They will perish, but you will endure; yes, they will all grow old like a garment; like a cloak you will change them, and they will be changed. But you are the same" (Psalm 102:26–27, my translation). God declares of himself, "I the LORD do not change," and it is precisely because of this that Israel can rest secure, since if God were capable of being changed by human action, Israel would already be consumed in his wrath (Malachi 3:6). Paul refers to the nations as exchanging the glory of a changeless, perfect God with that of a changing, imperfect deity (Romans 1:23).

Third, God has all knowledge and all power over every circumstance. There are no borders to God, no places where his sovereignty does not penetrate (Job 37:16). And God cannot err in what he knows. His knowledge is perfect: "Remember the former things of old; for I am God, and there is no other; I am God, and there is none like me, declaring the end from the beginning and from ancient times things not yet done, saying, 'My counsel shall stand, and I will accomplish all my purpose.... I have spoken, I will bring it to pass'" (Isaiah 46:9–11; cf. 42:9). Again, this comes to us as both threat and promise.

That God knows everything about us and has sovereign power over our destiny is bad news apart from a Mediator.

But in Christ, we are clothed in righteousness. God's knowledge has already accounted for all obstacles in the way of our salvation, and his power will conquer them. Paul writes, "In [Christ] we have obtained an inheritance, having been predestined according to the purpose of him who works all things according to the counsel of his will" (Ephesians 1:11). Our salvation is ultimately grounded in "God's purpose of election," says the apostle (Romans 9:11). "So then it depends not on human will or exertion, but on God, who has mercy" (9:16). Even Pharaoh is brought in by Paul as a material witness in this matter (9:17). God is sovereign over the whole "lump of clay"—humanity—to do what his wisdom ordains (9:11–24). Even the results of a throw of the dice are determined ultimately by God (Proverbs 16:33).

Fourth, God is *everywhere*, while transcending the very category of space itself. This means that he does not exercise his power, knowledge, and wisdom from afar but is so present in everything that he can bring about his intended results without in any way taking away the liberty or contingency of creatures. God is not "the Man Upstairs" who sometimes comes down when we pray hard enough. God is as present on the streets of New York City as he is in his heavens.

As we will see, especially when we come to the story of Job, these "invisible attributes" as Paul calls them in Romans 1:20, are not sufficient to arouse hope in the midst of crises, but they are essential presuppositions of it. Unless God is *God*, nothing else matters. We are *all* "without hope and without God in the world" (Ephesians 2:12 NIV), at least in any practical sense. We might as well adopt the Greek gods, who were little more than supercharged human beings.

While a weak God may make more sense in the light of our (interpreted) experience of suffering, it is not only at odds with Scripture but with hope. It may be of some momentary therapeutic usefulness to have a divine friend at one's side who merely feels our pain, but can one trust in, rely on, pray to, or praise a God who cannot or will not do anything about it? Even if we say that God *can* intervene but *refuses* to do so because of how highly he prizes our freedom, we face the same problems with God's character in the light of our experience. Is there anyone living who would say that God's refusal to intervene in the senseless carnage of the twentieth century, from World War I to Rwanda, is justified by his concern for our freedom from external control? Surely Scripture reveals God as intervening dramatically in human affairs in remarkably coercive ways in the past, so why not at Auschwitz? Surely the Jews' bondage in Egypt was not a greater evil, as we calculate such things, than the Holocaust. Is it really more of a comfort to tell its survivors that God willingly kept himself on the sidelines than to tell them that he works all things together for good (see Romans 8:28)? Surely we are faced with greater problems if we think of God as a bystander—perhaps not even knowing such evils ahead of time. This means we cannot even take comfort in God's having a larger plan and design for our tragedies in life. A random accident, the car accident that took the life of one's daughter, for example, is literally meaningless. How can one continue even to pray to a God like this? And if one were inclined to do so, what would it matter?

If one is trapped inside an elevator in a burning building, an outside fireman who can force the door open is preferable to a fellow victim who is also trapped but understands the problem. Being omniscient, God knows our pain and hears our cries. And in Christ, God did experience our human suffering inasmuch as he was the God-Man. But *as God*, he was able to rescue us because he possessed the very attributes that we do not possess. Because God is in himself invincible in power, wisdom, and knowledge, he cannot be hindered from bringing about the future he has promised.

Even the proud Babylonian King Nebuchadnezzar (whom former Iraqi dictator Saddam Hussein hailed as his predecessor) learned this lesson the hard way. One day, as Nebuchadnezzar walked along the roof of his palace, surveying his kingdom's glory and boasting in his success, God sent a wasting disease that transformed a great king into a peasant who lived like an animal. A humbled Nebuchadnezzar tells his own story:

> At the end of the days [of suffering] I, Nebuchadnezzar, lifted my eyes to heaven, and my reason returned to me, and I blessed the Most High, and praised and honored him who lives forever,
>
> for his dominion is an everlasting dominion,
>   and his kingdom endures from generation to generation;
> all the inhabitants of the earth are accounted as nothing,
>   and he does according to his will among the host of heaven
>   and among the inhabitants of the earth;
> and none can stay his hand
>   or say to him, "What have you done?"
>
> At the same time my reason returned to me, and for the glory of my kingdom, my majesty and splendor returned to me. My counselors and my lords sought me, and I was established in my kingdom, and still more greatness was added to me. Now I, Nebuchadnezzar, praise and extol and honor the King of heaven, for all his works are right and his ways are just; and those who walk in pride he is able to humble.

Daniel 4:34–37

So when God does act, it is out of strength, abundance, self-sufficiency, and freedom, not out of weakness, lack, dependence, or constraint.

Strong to Save

Although knowing these truths about God may not fully resolve our curiosities about the problem of evil and suffering, it is good news to those who are actually suffering. Our Father is strong to save. This means that he both *can* and *will* set everything right and wipe every tear from our eyes. This may not satisfy our reason or match our experience, but there is no other *practical* solution to the problem of evil and suffering than this.

We must eliminate both the idol of a loving but weak god and the idol of a strong but graceless god. Neither is great enough to capture the hearts and minds of our disenchanted age, especially in the face of evil, oppression, violence, and death. More importantly, neither vision represents the God of the Bible. The grand vision is found in the orthodox conception of the Trinity, where Jesus the Son reveals to us "God the Father, Almighty."

When Paul stood on Mars' hill, he took on both Epicurean and Stoic philosophers, the former basically deistic (pushing God out of sight so they could live irresponsibly), while the latter were basically pantheistic (identifying God with the creation). Ironically, given the typical criticism of the classical doctrine of God as too determined by Stoic elements, it is in this context (against Stoicism) that the Apostle to the Gentiles proclaimed Jesus and the resurrection, on the foundation that

> the God who made the world and everything in it is the Lord of heaven and earth and does not live in temples built by hands. And he is not served by human hands, as if he needed anything, because he himself gives all men life and breath and everything else. From one man he made every nation of men, that they should inhabit the whole earth; and he determined the times set for them and the exact places where they should live.

Acts 17:24–26 NIV

In other words, despite its idea of a static, unfeeling, unchanging deity, the Stoic view had collapsed Creator and creation in a manner quite similar to contemporary trends. It is the Christian doctrine of God, as maintained within historic Christianity, that invalidates both hyper-immanence (pantheism) and hyper-transcendence (deism). Jesus Christ not only teaches us but exhibits to us that the God of Israel is both the Lord over and beyond us and Immanuel, "God with us." God is not needy; we are. God is not dependent on us, but we are helpless without him. God determines the future, and therefore we can be confident that his suffering for us in Jesus Christ will yield the promised fruit: everlasting peace in a world where suffering is no more and God will be all in all.

chapter five
is anybody up there?

My wife, confined to bed rest not only by her pregnancy but by a severe hormone-induced depression, recited Psalm 51:12 as the cry of her heart: "Restore to me the joy of your salvation, and uphold me with a willing spirit." Never had she harbored the dark thoughts that now threatened to drown her in a sea of unbelief.

Unlike me, Lisa had in the past never really questioned God or his purposes. Although we were both nurtured in a similar Christian background, we handled trouble differently. She would be confused sometimes by the matter-of-fact way I would express my own opinions to God about how he was handling things, whining to God over the slightest disappointment.

But now the tables had turned: Lisa was in a deep, partly chemical but nevertheless real, depression. Whereas I was vocal in my pleas to God, Lisa became quiet, lonely, and angry. God seemed a million miles away — or actually maybe *too* close. He seemed to be actively putting her through trials, which caused her to question his goodness. If she allowed her experience to have the last word, she would give up all hope.

But God sustained her faith even when she could not. There was no obvious turning point, a particular day or week, that marked an observable transition from despair to hope. In fact, since we know from Scripture that we are *simultaneously* sinners and justified, doubters and believers, both were present all along. Lisa realized that she could not preach the Word to herself; she needed a herald sent from God himself to proclaim externally something different from what she felt internally. In times of crisis, the most important thing we can do is go to church. Chiefly, this is where God's herald announces that "external Word" that contradicts our private judgments. Working against the tide of our inner experience and thoughts, this announcement comes rushing toward us like water from the Himalayas: "You are forgiven; go in peace." It is also where Christ gives himself to us anew, sealing his fidelity to our salvation in his Supper, joining us with his saints' fellowship in invocation of his merciful presence, confession, prayer, and praise. Here we take our place, despite our misgivings, doubts, fears, and temptations, not with the scornful and proud, but with our fellow pilgrims.

Gradually, through a combination of factors (the end of the raging hormones after delivery, as well as wonder at simple truths made fresh in trial), she raised her eyes to heaven in gratitude again. With additional trials that come with the overwhelming challenges of premature triplets and a two-year-old, she learned, as I did, both the humiliation and treasure of dependence on God and those wonderful "masks" he wears when he comes to us through neighbors and the communion of saints.

Just as we cannot neatly separate the body and soul, we cannot untangle the threads of physical and spiritual depression or pain. Both are equally real, and they feed each other. That is why intense physical distress is often accompanied by spiritual doubts, and vice versa. At the heart of it all is the question of God's presence. Where is God when we need him most? Is anybody up there? Reading the circumstances of our own lives at times, much less the newspaper, we wonder. We would hardly be alive if we didn't.

In a real sense, God is *not* there—that is, he is not readily available to our experience. Long before medieval theologians were speculating about the *Deus absconditus* (the hidden God)—let alone radical theologians in recent times announcing the alleged "death of God"—the prophet Isaiah declared, "Truly You are God, who hide Yourself, O God of Israel, the Savior!" (Isaiah 45:15 NKJV). The Israelites' experience in exile had left them wondering whether God had turned his face from them, leaving them desolate and without his presence. The crises of the modern age have also shown the twentieth century that it did not have the theology to meet its gruesome match. The optimism of liberal theology extolled only a benevolent Providence that always blessed, never judged—the kind of "Providence" that gives an extra push now and then to human progress. Whether a result of philosophical speculation or personal experience (or, more likely, both), God's presence is no longer taken for granted in our age.

Even before the Holocaust, the "enlightened" age anticipated the despair that no longer surprises or dismays but is simply there, like an open wound one must learn to bear with no expectation of cure. In *The Birth of Tragedy* (1872), Friedrich Nietzsche introduced us to the classical myth of the gods Apollo and Dionysus. Apollo was a god of light, order, sanity; Dionysus a god of darkness, chaos, and insanity. While the former was the god of the heavens, the latter was the god of nature. While Apollo behaved himself and expected everyone to do so as well, Dionysus was the ribald and intoxicated deity who devoted himself to music and revelry.

Identifying with Dionysus rather than Apollo, Nietzsche and his disciples looked forward to the day when a superman would arrive, a Dionysian hero whose will to power would conquer the world. This person would stand in sharp contrast to the biblical God who, as a remnant of "inferior" Jewish mythology, had supposedly taught us to be weak and to accept our fate in this world. "The god on the cross is a curse on life, a signpost to seek redemption from life," but "Dionysus cut to pieces is a promise of life: it will be eternally reborn and return again from destruction."[1] In Nietzsche's writings, it was the madman who, first having sought God, eventually announced his death:

> "Whither is God?" he cried; "I will tell you. We have killed him, you and I. All of us are his murderers. But how did we do this? How could we drink up the sea? Who gave us the sponge to wipe away the entire horizon? What were we doing when we unchained this earth from its sun? Whither is it moving now? Whither are we moving? Away from all suns? Are we not plunging continually? Backward, sideward, forward, in all directions? Is there still any up or down? Are we not straying as through an infinite nothing? Do we not feel the breath of empty space? Has it not become colder? Is not night continually closing in on us? Do we not need to light lanterns in the morning?"[2]

The "death of God" leaves this world colder, less hospitable, and yet a vast, open expanse to be conquered by the supermen. Nietzsche at least had the character to step beyond a vapid, pedestrian deism and into the dark void.

It is no wonder, then, that Ludwig Feuerbach (1804–72) announced that "religion is the dream of the human mind," with God as nothing more than the projection of humanity.[3] For him, each of the doctrines of Christianity was an obstacle to humanity realizing its power and glorious destiny. "The Christian theory of justification by faith," he wrote, "is rooted in a cowardly renunciation of moral effort," and belief in the hereafter is nothing more than "an escape mechanism." Anticipating Marx, he concluded that religion was like a drug that kept people numb to reality.

But it was Nietzsche (1844–1900) who actually felt the burden to bring humanity the news of God's demise. Soon after, Sigmund Freud (1856–1939) turned this critique into a pseudoscientific theory, insisting that religion is nothing more than an illusion, a coping mechanism in the face of life's traumas. Combined with the pragmatism of William James, religion—especially in America—was now a form of therapy, a revelation of what we need (or think we need) rather than a revelation of God and our real need of him.

So, you see, long before the tragedies of our time, the modern age was preparing itself for life without God. We were not the first to wonder, "Is anybody up there?" The question of God's presence, his nearness, is especially acute when we're in trouble.

Hide Not Your Face from Us, O Lord

When Moses asked to see God's face, he was warned, "No one may see me and live" (Exodus 33:20 NIV). In fact, as the people of Israel arrived at Mount Sinai to receive the law, God told Moses to place limits around the mountain, "lest [the people] break through to gaze at the LORD" (Exodus 19:21 NKJV). So terrified were they of God's word, with the lightning, thunder, and smoke, that they begged that God speak no more (see 19:16–25; 20:18–21). Instead, they decided a few weeks later to fashion a golden calf, a more "seeker-friendly" version of God, one they could create and therefore control (see Exodus 32). The essence of idolatry is the fear of dealing with the true God, whose holiness fills us with fear because of our own sinfulness.

Thus, throughout biblical history (and history in general) there is this flight from the I AM, the God of power and glory. Our consciences testify to this God, but in our wickedness we try to suppress this awareness. We create a chasm and either plead ignorance (skepticism) or substitute projections of our own imagination or felt needs (idolatry). We build suitable projections of gods who will not threaten us, gods who are too far away to cause any harm, or, if they are friendly and useful enough, gods who are close at hand, gods who do not judge. Indeed, they are projections of ourselves (see Romans 1 and 2). To that extent, Feuerbach, Marx, Nietzsche, and Freud have more on the ball than many modern theologians. Religion actually *is* a projection of our own felt needs, fig leaves of our inner lives to cloak our guilt, a golden calf of our own imaginations to hide us from the God of blinding glory. But religion is not revelation. Religion expresses *our* longings; revelation communicates *God's*.

After Israel's disobedience at Sinai, God's presence remained a problem. That sounds strange, doesn't it? We usually think the real problem when it comes to belief in God is *atheism*—in other words, the absence of God. But the Israelites' actual encounter with the God of revelation demonstrates that there is also a problem raised by his existence and, more specifically, his *presence*. If God maintains his presence among his sinful people, he will very likely break out in wrath against them. Yes, but then the world will say that God led Israel out of Egypt only to let his people die in the desert, Moses argues in Exodus 32. So God maintains his presence, but "outside the camp," in a pitched tent where his glory is hidden behind a curtain.

Religion, especially in its upbeat mode, assumes that everything is fine between God and us (this was Israel's original assumption until he actually spoke). We're basically good people, and God is only capable of love anyway. We have God on our side! But revelation upsets this nice picture. God's presence is a danger as well as a blessing. There needs to be distance.

Eventually, after God led his people into the Promised Land, Solomon built the majestic temple, and the Glory Cloud filled this earthly sanctuary of God's presence. Once a year, the high priest would enter with the sacrificial blood and sprinkle it on the mercy seat, laying his hands on the head of a scapegoat to transfer Israel's guilt to the animal, sending it into the wilderness. But as Israel's sins grew greater and she turned from Yahweh to the gods of the nations, the Glory Cloud left the temple, as it had in Eden, and once again God's sanctuary was taken back up into heaven. He hid his face from Israel, and she would soon go into captivity.

It was in this atmosphere that Isaiah was raised up as a prophet. Although God had hidden his face from the house of Jacob, Isaiah and the remnant would hope in him (see Isaiah 8:17): "'With a little wrath I hid My face from you for a moment; but with everlasting kindness I will have mercy on you,' says the LORD, your Redeemer" (Isaiah 54:8 NKJV). God's nearness and distance were metaphorically revealed in spatial terms (in other words, near/far, above/below), but the point is the qualitative distinction between Creator and creature: "'For My thoughts are not your thoughts, nor are your ways My ways,' says the LORD. 'For as the heavens are higher than the earth, so are My ways higher than your ways, and My thoughts than your thoughts'" (Isaiah 55:8–9 NKJV).

The Israelites needed to learn that their "hidden God" could not be seen: "for no one may see me and live." If, being sinners, they were to be saved, they must learn to receive God as he revealed himself through his Word. Turning away from false religions, the Israelites must ignore their own imaginations, speculations, and experiences as the ground for their faith and practice, relying only on the promise of the gospel and following the precepts of God's law. Thus, even in exile, far from the temple and the land of promise, the remnant enjoyed God's merciful presence in far greater measure than the adulterous generation had known in Israel.

But Why Is God Hiding?

God is everywhere, isn't he? Don't we believe in his omnipresence? To be sure, God is Spirit, and the cosmos cannot contain him (2 Chronicles 2:6). But does that really help us where we are right now? This is equivalent to trying to prove God's existence. So what if we are able to demonstrate God's sheer presence? So what if "in the rustling grass [we] hear him pass ," and "he speaks to [us] everywhere," as one hymn puts it? The real question is: What is he *saying*? Do we experience his presence as an approaching conqueror or as a liberator? Do we hear him confirming the judgment of conscience against us or as the redeemer and justifier of the ungodly? Where is God *for* us, *on our side*? God's presence is at best ambiguous, at worst, terrifying, apart from the gospel.

Even Nietzsche got this point: It is irrelevant that a god merely "exists" and is omnipresent, an incomprehensible transcendence. Even if a "heavenly realm" existed, "it is certain that knowledge of it would be the most useless of all knowledge."[4] So what if there is this "other world" inhabited by God? Even if his presence fills the earth, how could this mean anything to us in our experience? The ugly ditch becomes a grand canyon.

But for Israel, it was not simply about the philosophical problem of God's transcendence (distance) and immanence (nearness), but about the *ethical* ditch, which really *is* ugly. The sheer presence or existence of God is not itself good news to us in our sin. If we were inherently righteous, faithful in all ways to God's holy will, the announcement of God's omnipresence would be good news. But Adam and Eve did not see it that way. After they had sinned, they fled from God's presence, that localized presence they used to enjoy; the Holy of Holies was the whole garden itself, without a curtain to separate the royal couple from their Creator. Similarly, when the Israelites heard God speak his law in majestic holiness at Mount Sinai, though at first curious to catch a glimpse of the eye of the storm (God in his majestic glory), they begged God to be silent.

News of God's majesty, power, glory, holiness, and justice only comforts those who are not guilty. This is why God *mercifully* denies Moses the request to see the divine Majesty, but condescends to show him his "backward parts" — that is, his goodness and mercy, by preaching a sermon: "I will proclaim my name, Yahweh. I will have mercy on whom I will have mercy" (Exodus 33:19, my translation).

As Adam and Eve were redeemed only after God, the one true Seeker, caught up with them and proclaimed the gospel, stripping them of their fig leaves only to clothe them in sacrificial skins, so the Israelites were only calmed and comforted by the Holy Presence when they knew that the high priest was interceding on their behalf with the blood sprinkled on the mercy seat. We will see in our discussion of Job's life how God's presence can be a burden — a threat. Those who recognize God as righteous, holy and just, glorious in power and might, and themselves as none of these, can easily (and correctly!) correlate God's presence with judgment and punishment. Apart from God's goodness, announced to us supremely in the gospel, we can only respond to God's presence with fear — that is, if we have not yet sufficiently suppressed the truth in our unrighteousness.

The theologian of glory, said Martin Luther, sees God everywhere and in everything. God shows up everywhere, and it is always a happy occasion. But haven't we already affirmed God's omnipresence — that he is everywhere? Yes, but that is not what

Luther and the other Reformers were criticizing. What Luther and John Calvin meant was this: For those who seek an unmediated, direct encounter with the God of Glory, it is enough that "the heavens declare the glory of God" (Psalm 19:1). For such a theology they do not need a special revelation of God in the gospel, because, as Paul himself says in the first chapters of Romans, even pagans know there is a God simply by the demonstration of nature. They only think that they can contemplate the majesty of God without fear, because they do not really know themselves very well. But for those who know themselves to be helpless sinners—guilty and under God's just sentence—this is hardly comforting.

Calvin makes this point in the very beginning of his *Institutes*.[5] All of the starlit nights, summer breezes, moving symphonies, dramatic demonstrations, and visible testimonies to God's glory—shining "like burning lamps"—only confirm our conscience in its verdict against us. A dazzling symphony or a moving sunset may fill one with awe and wonder at the grandeur of the universe—the starry heavens above and the moral law within, as philosopher Immanuel Kant expressed the two most undeniable truths. But none of this answers the question: Where is God *for me*, *for us*, given the mess we are in right now? There is no comfort in knowing that God is "everywhere" in the abstract unless I know that he is nearby *for my good*, and not in order to execute a sentence that my conscience knows to be just. Until that is settled, no general knowledge of God from his visible works will bring me to any place except despair.

The glory of God testifies to God's existence and perfection, but it does not testify to God's interest in saving me. It cannot *reconcile* me to God. It does not announce the justification of the ungodly, but simply the majesty of God and our own smallness among the works of God (see Psalm 8). For a revelation of God's *saving* will, more than the visible realm of nature is needed. I need a promise, and not a general promise but a particular promise addressed to me: "I have forgiven your sins, so come to me. Do not be afraid." Otherwise, being in God's presence is a dangerous enterprise.

Although the psalmist will meditate on God's works in creation and redemption, he confesses, "Your way was in the sea, Your path in the great waters, and Your footsteps were not known" (Psalm 77:19 NKJV). This is crucial for our trials, because of how prone we are to interpret (or try to interpret) God's footsteps in providence. Mystics and rationalists revel in this abyss. Instead of regarding it as God's hiddenness, into which God warned the Israelites not to gaze, they invest great energy and enthusiasm in probing, speculating, opining, experiencing, imagining. However, the God they meet at the other end is the consuming fire. One moment we may be lost in the grandeur and sheer force of the ocean's waves; the next we are just as lost in their dread as they burst their bonds, causing havoc and devastation.

God hides those who trust in him under the shadow of his wings (Psalm 17:8), but he also hides his face from his enemies (Psalm 10:11). After his great sin, the psalmist begs God not to hide his face from him (Psalm 51:11). God is a hiding place (Psalm 32:7), and yet when he comes in wrath, the inhabitants of the earth will cry out for the rocks to fall on them in order to hide them from his glorious appearing (Revelation 6:16). So he is both a hiding place and a place from which we hide ourselves. God is both our greatest problem and solution. His presence is the worst news or the best news, the most fearful threat or the most cheerful comfort. From Genesis to Revelation, there is this struggle, this awkwardness, ranging from indescribable joy to utter terror, when we talk about God's presence or face.

This is far indeed from the modern triviality with which we treat this subject. We assume that God is near, and that this is necessarily good news, without needing to hear anything more said. Or when we are tormented by life's circumstances, we assume that God is far away, when in fact, as the cross itself demonstrates and Paul attests in his own suffering, it is precisely there and then when God is closest. That's the paradox. Our experience is simply wrong. Things are not as they seem. God is most intimately involved in our lives often when we least experience him. Such contradictions of our ordinary experience are abundant even in the natural sciences. It was perfectly understandable that people once upon a time thought that the earth was flat, the sun and the moon were roughly the same size, and the earth was the center of the universe: after all, this matches the most universal experience of ordinary people. However, we know better now, because more thorough and sophisticated analysis has challenged such commonly held notions. How much more likely it is, then, that our ordinary experience of God and his ways can be challenged by his own revelation!

So God's presence is ambiguous without the gospel. How do we know we will not hear the same word spoken through Amos?

> *Woe to you who desire the day of the LORD! For what good is the day of the LORD to you? It will be darkness, and not light. It will be as though a man fled from a lion only to meet a bear! Or as though he went into his house for safety only to lean his hand on the wall, and a scorpion bit him! Is not the day of the LORD darkness, and not light? Is it not very dark, with no brightness in it?*
>
> Amos 5:18–20, my translation

What makes us think that God's appearing is good news for us? At least Nietzsche knew himself better than most of us know ourselves today. He knew that someone had to go — either God or himself. He would not entertain the third possibility:

that God was present to *save*. He would not concede that he, a superman, *needed* saving, so he could only conclude that God's presence meant death for himself. Nietzsche conceded that this was the cause of his madness, and he did in fact die insane, but there was nowhere else to hide.

The Secret Things Belong to the Lord

The Preacher says, "Do not be rash with your mouth, and let not your heart utter anything hastily before God. For God is in heaven, and you on earth" (Ecclesiastes 5:2 NKJV). Some bold souls who forget this try to storm heaven's gates and search God's secret chambers. "God told me to move to Kansas," they then announce. "God gave me a revelation for you." "God will heal your son." This is the sort of thing against which God commanded Jeremiah to warn Israel, and essentially the charge against the "false prophets" is that they have used God instead of confining themselves to his word:

> *I did not send the prophets, yet they ran; I did not speak to them, yet they prophesied.... Am I a God at hand, declares the LORD, and not a God afar off?... Behold, I am against the prophets, declares the LORD, who use their tongues and declare, "declares the LORD." Behold, I am against those who prophesy lying dreams, declares the LORD, and who tell them and lead my people astray by their lies and their recklessness.*

> Jeremiah 23:21, 23, 31 – 32

Even when we discuss God's gracious election, our natural curiosity leads us to inquire beyond the sacred page. After discussing predestination, the apostle Paul cries out in praise instead of speculation:

> *Oh, the depth of the riches both of the wisdom and knowledge of God! How unsearchable are His judgments*

and His ways past finding out! "For who has known the mind of the LORD? Or who has become His counselor?" "Or who has first given to Him and it shall be repaid to him?" For of Him and through Him and to Him are all things, to whom be glory forever. Amen.

Romans 11:33 – 36 NKJV

John Calvin reminds us, "Human curiosity renders the discussion of predestination, already somewhat difficult of itself, very confusing and even dangerous. No restraints can hold it back from wandering in forbidden bypaths and thrusting upward to the heights. If allowed, it will leave no secret to God that it will not search out and unravel."[6] This is why Calvin insisted that, instead of seeking out God's secret predestination, we must contemplate Christ, in whom we are chosen and in whom God is revealed as our Savior.

We do not know what God has decided in his deep and mysterious hiddenness, and we can only know what God condescends to reveal to us as he cloaks his unapproachable light in humility and weakness. We cannot climb up to God, but he has descended to us. This is the gospel in a nutshell, and it sustains us in suffering. When we cannot climb the first rung, when the flame of faith is barely a flicker, our Savior descends to carry us through the valley of the shadow of death.

It is God who must take initiative to reveal himself. He does this in creation, but in this natural revelation he is still hidden. We can know him as Power, Majesty, Governor, Wise Creator, Providence, and Judge, but of what good is this knowledge when we are in the grip of our personal and collective sinfulness, living this side of Eden? When we encounter great trials and temptations, our conscience (like our experience) accuses us, but the word of the gospel brings God as close as the sounds of the preacher's voice (Romans 10:8).

"The Harvest Is Past, the Summer Is Ended, and We Are Not Saved"

In the fullness of time, "the Word became flesh and dwelt [literally, "pitched his tent"] among us" (John 1:14). In the incarnation, that same Word who spoke from the unapproachable mountain of smoke and tempest became a particular Jewish man in history. Instead of coming in power, glory, judgment, and blinding light, he came in weakness, humiliation, and suffering. In Jesus Christ, the God-Man, the true temple is rebuilt after its destruction. It is his body torn from top to bottom, like the veil of Herod's temple, that gives us access through his blood into the Holy of Holies. Both the High Priest and the Victim, he is God's Presence in mercy toward us rather than in judgment and destruction.

But still we can say in our exile, with Israel, "The harvest is past, the summer is ended, and we are not saved" (Jeremiah 8:20). Even after the cross and resurrection, we are still waiting for the consummation of God's kingdom. Peter writes,

> *Beloved, I now write to you this second epistle ... that you may be mindful of the words which were spoken before by the holy prophets, and of the commandment of us, the apostles of the Lord and Savior, knowing this first: that scoffers will come in the last days, walking according to their own lusts, and saying, "Where is the promise of His coming? For since the fathers fell asleep, all things continue as they were from the beginning of creation."... The Lord is not slack concerning His promise, as some count slackness, but is longsuffering toward us, not willing that any should perish but that all should come to repentance.*
>
> 2 Peter 3:1–4, 9 NKJV

We do not help others or ourselves in times of crisis when we fail to realize that there is more to salvation than we have yet experienced. Our destiny is secured, but this does not make us immune to the tragedies that mark our pilgrim way.

Even the apparent absence of God in this in-between time is the very opposite of what it appears to be to the world — or to our own unbaptized experience, catechized by the world to believe that tragedies have no clear origin (except perhaps in political missteps) and therefore no hope of being part of a master plan. Faced with injustice, rapacity, poverty, cruelty, suffering, and unrelenting news of crisis, our age thinks that God, if there is such a being, has taken a long vacation. And, we have to admit, it looks like that on the surface of things. We rarely hear about a massacre in a remote village or a devastating earthquake and conclude a week later, "Oh, now we understand why God allowed it." It almost never makes sense — and that is fine, because we are not God. We do not need to add to the insult of tragedy the injury of expecting people to discern something that might make the event more rational or acceptable. Without the announcement of the gospel in special revelation — without reading nature and history in the light of Christ — natural revelation, including human experience, would *not* conclude that there *is* a gracious God.

Actually, if God were to prove the scoffers wrong immediately, they would not have the opportunity to repent. It is his patience, says Peter, that keeps his judgment at bay. Whenever we wonder why God does not act in the world to end this or that injustice, let us ask ourselves whether we have *thanked* God for not *yet* bringing about the judgment that will make everything right and undo the evil to which we have contributed in our own way. Are we grateful that he is patiently enduring evil and suffering for the very sake of people such as us, who would otherwise have been on the receiving end of his swift justice? Now that we are safely in the ark, are we so eager to have the door closed on our loved ones and neighbors? The renewal of all things and the end of pain will be preceded by the last judgment. While we do indeed wait eagerly for the age to come, we revel also in God's patience, that in-between time in which God graciously draws sinners to himself.

An important implication of this truth is that through this revelation of the reason why God allows this evil age to continue, we are able not only to hold on to hope that evil will be eradicated; we are also able to participate in the divine reconciliation even of those (like us) who *perpetrate* suffering. In Christ, there is a place for the instigators, as well as the victims, to be saved. The very scoffers who exploit the delay of judgment in order to advance their oppression, violence, and injustice can be brought to repentance through the proclamation of God's Word.

And they can be prepared for that Word by God's Spirit through the imperfect community that Christ is forming to reflect his own reconciling purpose. One thinks of John M. Perkins, an African-American minister working for social justice, and Tommy Tarrants, a former Ku Klux Klansman, who coauthored *He's My Brother* (1994) on the power of the gospel to bring about racial reconciliation. In the church where I am a member, made up mostly of postwar Dutch immigrants and their children, there are remarkable stories of Jews who came to faith in the Messiah while they were hidden in the homes of ordinary Christians who risked their own lives. Yet even more redolent of God's gracious patience in delaying justice, some of those stories include the conversion of Nazi soldiers and officers as well.

The delay of the last judgment and therefore of final rest from war, disease, violence, injustice, and pain is not just Muzak playing in the background on the telephone when we're put on hold. It is a *productive* delay that is itself the space in which God is fulfilling his redemptive purposes. Therefore, we must not see those who perpetrate evil as the condemned but as those who may be brought to repentance, just as we have been. While there is an earthly justice to which evildoers must be brought, this is neither the time nor the place for us to execute God's final justice, as the "Sons of Thunder" learned the hard way when Jesus rebuked them (Luke 9:51–56). James and John wanted to come in power and glory to judge, while Jesus came on this mission in weakness and grace.

Let us never forget that when the world saw God at his weakest moment—the Father hiding his face from the humiliated and guilt-laden Son—God was performing his greatest act of redemption, beside which the exodus pales in comparison. And so, even now, where the world can only see God's absence, we, by faith, see God's saving presence. As Jesus told Paul, "My grace is sufficient for you, for My strength is made perfect in weakness" (2 Corinthians 12:9 NKJV). Peter tells us that while the world recognizes only another opportunity to scoff at God's apparent absence, the church sees this as God's loving nearness.

The world in its unbelief should not long for God's presence and justice, because when he does appear this second time, it will be in glory and judgment. But for now the church sees God's presence hidden under the form of absence, bringing the lost to a saving sight of the Crucified by the preached cross: "For Jews request a sign, and Greeks seek after wisdom; but we preach Christ crucified, to the Jews a stumbling block and to the Greeks foolishness" (1 Corinthians 1:22–23 NKJV). Just when it looks as if God has taken a long vacation from the world, he has been and is still actually busy building his kingdom, and even the gates of hell will not be able to withstand this mighty work. Behind the scenes he is reconciling the wicked to himself and to each other.

Thus, Feuerbach's conviction that in religion "to enrich God, man must become poor; that God may be all, man must be nothing,"[7] is turned on its head: "For you know the grace of our Lord Jesus Christ, that though He was rich, yet for your sakes He became poor, that you through His poverty might become rich" (2 Corinthians 8:9 NKJV).

Is this story of God's triumph through tragedy, power through weakness, wisdom through foolishness, not sufficient to comfort us when our conscience, heart, and mind condemn us? And if God's presence in saving mercy is so powerful in weakness at the cross, so active in the very moment it looks as if there is nobody up there, surely we can trust God to be most present in our own lives when everything within us would convince us that he is the least present: when we are suffering, when we are being treated unfairly, when we fail God miserably, and when we are tired and lonely in the world. Like their Greek forebears, the philosophers of our age may find such a message "foolishness," a crutch for the weak, "the opiate of the people." But to those who are called, both Jews and Greeks, Christ is the power of God and the wisdom of God. Because "the foolishness of God is wiser than men, and the weakness of God is stronger than men" (1 Corinthians 1:25 NKJV), those who seek to hold on to their life will lose it, while those who give up their life will find it.

At last, "the broad, ugly ditch" is crossed, not by us but by God. God has built a bridge to us in the person and work of the God-Man. While we cannot leap across it or pull God down out of heaven by our rational, moral, or emotional strength, God has come down to us. Not only has he become human, suffered in our place, and been raised to life as the down payment on our own resurrection; he comes to us now in the ministry of Word and Sacrament. Paul writes,

> *But the righteousness of faith speaks in this way, "Do not say in your heart, 'Who will ascend into heaven?'"*
> *(that is, to bring Christ down from above) or, "'Who will*

descend into the abyss?'" (that is, to bring Christ up from the dead). But what does it say? "The word is near you, in your mouth and in your heart" (that is, the word of faith which we preach): that if you confess with your mouth the Lord Jesus and believe in your heart that God has raised Him from the dead, you will be saved.

Romans 10:6–9 NKJV

At long last, God's presence among us is forever only good news, filling our hearts with delight instead of terror. Comforted by the cross, let us turn away from the theologies of glory we find all around us: in the signs and wonders so many demand; in the clamor for success, numbers, and popularity in this world; in the speculative, mystical, and subjectivist trends of our time; and in the triumphalism that so marks the contemporary church. Content to die with Christ, we have been raised in his new life. Christ's will to weakness is stronger than modern humanity's will to power, and that which the supermen of our age regard as opium for the masses is "the power of God to salvation for everyone who believes" (Romans 1:16 NKJV).

chapter six
if we just knew why
GOD let it happen

The day after Christmas 2004, a massive tsunami triggered by an earthquake in the Indian Ocean claimed the lives of approximately 200,000 people. The whole earth seemed to echo with one collective gasp, demanding, "Why, God?" According to a CBS News report, "In India, a leading Hindu priest explained that the disaster was caused by 'huge pent-up man-made evil on earth' and the positions of the planets. Israeli chief rabbi Shlomo Amar proclaimed, 'The world is being punished for wrong-doing.'"[1] According to a number of Muslim clerics, the tsunami was divine judgment not on the faithful Muslims, who made up the largest percentage of victims, but on the scantily clad "Christian" tourists who were corrupting the beaches. On the other hand, liberal clergy of all stripes were just as dogmatic in their pronouncement that God had nothing to do with the tragedy. Either we know exactly what God is doing (usually punishing specific people for specific sins), or we deny that God is in charge of the world. Similar views were exchanged in the aftermath of Hurricanes Katrina and Rita in 2005. These two extremes seem to be all too common expressions when crises strike, on a global or personal scale.

In the first book I edited, former Surgeon General C. Everett Koop contributed a chapter recounting his investigation of a famous faith healer.[2] Attending one of the evangelist's meetings, Koop followed up on some of the "healed" individuals. In one case, an elderly man was introduced to the crowd as blind. The evangelist gave him a large-print Bible, which, under the bright lights, he was able to read, however haltingly. To dramatize the alleged miracle, the evangelist took off the man's glasses and smashed them on the stage. Returning to his poorly lit apartment, the elderly gentleman not only found he could not *read* his Bible, but he could barely *find* it, since he no longer had his glasses. In that chapter, Koop challenged the faith-healing industry and encouraged readers to recover a fresh sense of wonder and appreciation for God's ordinary providence, working through doctors and natural processes that God himself created and upholds.

Why do we look for God only in the miraculous? Why do we associate God's activity in our lives with a spectacular disappearance of a medically documented tumor but are not as ready to acknowledge the same in its reduction over time through radiation or surgery? Is God not as much the healer when a wound recovers gradually through various human means as when he miraculously intervenes?

My goal in this chapter is to help us recover this appreciation for God's activity in our lives and in history through ordinary providence, that government he exercises in Christ and by his Spirit, which is largely unseen and unknown to us but nevertheless essential to our flourishing. The assumption I would like to challenge is that God is limited to the miraculous. This misunderstanding often takes two apparently opposite forms: either the belief that God has somehow obligated himself to heal us miraculously or the view that whenever suffering comes, it is a direct and immediate action of God. In both cases, the confidence that God works through means and the ordinary processes he himself created and sustains — in other words, our belief in providence — is undermined. Furthermore, it assumes a view of divine action that eliminates or trivializes the actions of human beings, weather patterns, and other created factors that have their own prescribed freedom under God.

Like Job's counselors, well-meaning brothers and sisters sometimes encourage us to try to discern what God is up to in a given tragedy or what he is trying to teach us. They assume God is *directly* causing our suffering in order to do something to or for us that will bring him glory and us an ultimate good. Since this sounds so close to the truth, it is vital to use an entire chapter to try to sort this out from the Scriptures. While God is ultimately sovereign over all events, large and small, and will not allow us to endure a trial that he cannot turn to our profit, a lot of the adversities we face in this life are simply part of the web of ordinary causes and effects in the world. Upon learning that one has cancer, the first reaction should not be to think as if God had pointed his finger in the victim's direction and shouted, "Cancer!" Nor should we think God is uninvolved — perhaps caught off guard himself with the bad news. God has arranged a world in which he neither controls everything *directly* (that is, apart from means) nor is just another member of creation who could himself be overwhelmed by the course of events.

When we think of trials as direct, immediate "acts of God" rather than as consequences of a complicated network of secondary causes over which God is ultimately sovereign and therefore capable of working into a gracious design, their meaning is assumed to be obvious. On top of the suffering itself, one is supposed to be able also to read God's mind to some degree and is expected to see all difficulties, not as they appear outwardly, but as opportunities to learn something. This can trivialize not only the troubles of the sufferer but of his or her loved ones, who are also suffering in their own way. While I trust God's word that he was doing something to and for me through my father's anguish, I did not know what it was then or now, and I am not sure I will in the future. I might, but I might not. At least in the middle of the crisis, the big thing on my mind was what my father was going through, not how I could turn it into my own learning experience.

The last thing at least some believers need in their trials is the added burden of trying to figure out why it is all happening. And the good news here is that nowhere in Scripture are we expected to do that. God's secrets remain just that. We must try to avoid two extremes: one, suggesting that God's secret purposes in our lives and in providence generally are *available* to us; and the other, usually in reaction, concluding that God does not actually *have* a purpose for all of the details of our lives, from the smallest to the greatest.

The "Two Books" of God

A brief mention should first be made as to how we arrived at the false dilemma of either thinking that God is directly and immediately the cause of every circumstance or else the view that he is relatively uninvolved.

Although the medieval theologian Thomas Aquinas offered a sound treatment of God's providence in terms of *concursus*—that is, God's sovereign governance of all creaturely affairs precisely in and through secondary (or natural) means—the popular religion of the age waxed increasingly superstitious. Death was all around, and eventually the Plague, also known as the "Black Death," claimed nearly a third of Europe's population. The people wanted assurances that they were not simply helpless victims. They wanted to be able to control their fate, and so they often appealed to magic the way some today use crystals, repeat various mantras, adopt the latest spiritual formula, or entrust their hopes to TV evangelists. The medieval world was "enchanted" with good forces and evil forces, they believed, and this often made it difficult for the emerging sciences, particularly medicine, to achieve success in the popular imagination.

The Reformation of the sixteenth century, however, challenged superstition. Instead of busying ourselves with the hidden, unseen world, we should concentrate on the world that is known to us, either by what God has revealed in nature (and is therefore open to scientific investigation) or else in Scripture. Nature and Scripture were even referred to as the "two books" of God. The Reformers referred to common, everyday events as signs of God's ordinary presence and work in the world. If a scientist discovers a cure for a particular disease, they said, we should see such a person as a "mask" of God—in other words, as a human instrument in God's hands to provide for us in our affliction. Even the baker is such a "mask" through whom God answers our prayer for daily bread.

But in the Enlightenment era, the West rejected not only the pope but Scripture as well. Only that which our reason or experience could determine could count as truth. The "two books" were reduced to one, and the distinction between God's ordinary (providential) and extraordinary (miraculous) activity in the world was transformed into a denial of both. Not only was the latter reduced to the former; providence itself (although the term was still used) was now a barren "nature" devoid of any supernatural purpose or sovereign involvement. God was needed in the beginning, to get things started, but it all runs now pretty much on its own. In Isaac Newton's view of things, it is all a giant cosmic machine. God became the ideal modern monarch: cutting ribbons, kissing babies, symbolizing our values and aspirations, but pretty much staying out of our way.

In reaction against this, Romanticism and spiritualism have returned to something more like medieval superstition. This has affected us profoundly. Today, we are often forced to choose between naturalism and hyper-supernaturalism. That is to say, either God takes a backseat to science—the real provider for all our needs—or we can only believe that his hand is present where we see it present, namely, in the miraculous. The idea that God provides for us through ordinary, natural, relatively reliable creatures and processes has been largely lost, at least in mainstream culture. Either God works *spectacularly* or *rarely*, if at all. We recognize the hyper-supernaturalism, for example, when brothers and sisters seem frozen in their tracks by a momentous (or sometimes even trivial) decision, waiting for an obvious sign from the Lord—a "leading" or some direct revelation of his will.

Distinctions That Make a Difference

I believe that a renewed appreciation for God's providential care requires that we affirm the following distinctions and uphold both equally.

Things Hidden and Things Revealed

"The secret things belong to the LORD our God, but the things that are revealed belong to us and to our children forever, that we may do all the words of this law" (Deuteronomy 29:29). This distinction between things hidden and things revealed is maintained throughout Scripture. In fact, the exact form that the fulfillment of Old Testament prophecy would take in the unfolding plan of redemption is called "a secret and hidden wisdom of God, which God decreed before the ages for our glory," and which now has been "revealed to us through the Spirit" in the gospel (1 Corinthians 2:7, 10). This response was elicited after an assault on Paul's ministry by certain "super-apostles" who felt they had a higher form of knowledge than he did. These "super-apostles" claimed to have cracked the combination to God's heavenly safe. To their claim to *private* knowledge (*gnosis*), Paul lifted up the *public* knowledge available in the Word of God entrusted to him and the other apostles, which was the revelation of God's plan of salvation in the fullness of time. This revealed knowledge has to do with God's character, purposes, and will for our redemption in Christ, culminating in God's everlasting glory. It was open to everyone as historical truth, as cosmic revelation, and not a private truth about what will happen to this or that person.

Although God has revealed much more in this new covenant era than he did in the old covenant era, he has still not revealed everything. In fact, Scripture never indicates that we will ever know everything or have all our questions answered. God has revealed everything we need to know but not everything we might like to know. He remains Lord over his counsels. We know he has decreed all that comes to pass (see, for example, Psalm 139:16; Proverbs 16:4, 33; Acts 13:48; 17:26; Ephesians 1:4–5; 2:10), but we lack any promise that we can access this information through proper formulae. In fact, the attempt to know more than God has actually revealed is characteristic of superstition and magic rather than of Christian piety.

What then of Romans 12:2, which promises that "by testing you may discern what is the will of God, what is good and acceptable and perfect"? As usual, we must read this verse in context: "Do not be conformed to this world, but be transformed by the renewal of your mind, that by testing you may discern what is the will of God, what is good and acceptable and perfect." In other words, we must immerse ourselves in the study of Scripture, which renews our minds and allows us to test ourselves — that is, to investigate our beliefs and practices by God's Word. In so doing, we are able to know God's will better — not his secret will, which remains hidden from us, but his good and perfect will as it is revealed in Scripture. That is why Paul refers us to God's Word for this knowledge and not to "hunches," "leadings," "promptings," and "signs." God's good and perfect will is not secret. It is not hidden from us, in the way his eternal decrees are hidden. We have no reason to believe that God will specially and supernaturally reveal to us whom we should marry or which job we should take or where we should live, even though we know that he has "determined allotted periods and the boundaries of [our] dwelling place" (Acts 17:26). Yet we can and should be confident that he has revealed everything necessary for salvation and godliness.

This in no way downplays God's sovereignty over or interest in the minutest details of our lives. Few have written more eloquently or forcefully for God's secret predestination than John Calvin. And yet he also says,

All things may be ordained by God's plan, according to a sure dispensation, [but] for us they are fortuitous. Not that we think that fortune rules the world and men, tumbling all things at random up and down, for it is fitting that this folly be absent from the Christian's breast! But since the order, reason, end, and necessity of those things which happen for the most part lie hidden in God's purpose, and are not apprehended by human opinion, those things, which it is certain take place by God's will, are in a sense fortuitous. For they bear on the face of them no other appearance, whether they are considered in their own nature or weighed according to our knowledge and judgment.[3]

Earlier, Calvin declares that "it would not even be useful for us to know what God himself ... willed to be hidden." Recalling a retort reported by Augustine, he adds, "When a certain shameless fellow mockingly asked a pious old man what God had done before the creation of the world, the latter aptly countered that he had been building hell for the curious."[4] Like Augustine, Calvin was simply following Scripture in humbly accepting God's majesty, which allows God to keep his own secrets.

Common Grace and Saving Grace

This is another crucial distinction to bear in mind when we are considering God's ways in the world. Just as we too often limit God's activity to the miraculous, we easily limit it to the redemptive. We see God's hand in the exodus, in leading Israel into the Promised Land, in the person and work of Christ, in sending the Spirit, and in the life of the church — but what about God's hand in preserving the world after the fall? What about protecting Cain after he had murdered Abel? We recognize God's hand in Jerusalem, but what about Babylon and Rome? And yet if we confuse God's common grace (corresponding to providence) and redeeming grace (corresponding to miracle), we can make the opposite mistake of thinking that God's providential concern in the world, restraining evil and wickedness so that some degree of good can flourish, is itself saving.

Civil religion is an obvious example of this, if we think God's "shining city on a hill" is America rather than the heavenly Zion. Just as we have to avoid the extremes of either denying God's providence altogether or making all of God's activity miraculous, we have to avoid confusing God's gracious care for the world in all of its rebellion with his plan of redeeming a people for himself in Christ. Distinguishing *and* upholding both is a difficult but necessary task if we are to rightly understand the biblical meaning of God's providence.

Presbyterian theologian John Murray has claimed justly, concerning the doctrine of common grace, that "on this question Calvin not only opened a new vista but also a new era in theological formulation."[5] Although the term itself came into use much later, the treatment of what we now call "common grace" fell under Calvin's discussion of God's providence.

As Christians, we naturally think of the Holy Spirit's work in the lives of believers. This perception is understandable, given the sheer proportion of biblical passages that treat it in that context. And yet we must not overlook the fact that the same Spirit who brooded over the waters in creation upholds all things (along with the Father and the Son) and is just as active in lavishing his gifts of intelligence, friendship, love, passion, vocation, family, culture, government, art, science, and so forth on non-Christians as he is in lavishing his saving gifts on his people.

Just as some Christians demand God's direct involvement in their lives to the point of presuming to be able to discern his secret plans, some Christians expect Scripture to address every possible contingency of their lives. But while we must limit our "thus says the Lord" to what God has actually said (now laid down in Scripture), we must not limit our pursuit of truth, goodness, and beauty merely to the pages of Scripture. The reality of God's common grace means we are free to pursue—and indeed expected to pursue—truth, goodness, and beauty wherever God's Spirit has scattered it, even in secular sources.

In other words, we must reject the false dichotomy that assumes God either directly reveals our every step or God does not order our steps at all. We must remember that, while Scripture leads us into infallible truth even on points that overlap with common grace, God has given gifts to all people, believers and unbelievers alike, which we must capitalize on in a variety of earthly callings and pursuits.

As Murray points out, common grace accounts for a variety of benefits that God gives to all people, indiscriminately. First, it restrains sin. In the aftermath of September 11, Christians have been asked, once again, to address the problem of evil. While acknowledging evil's mysteriousness, part of my response to those requests has included a question for the questioner, namely, "How do you explain the problem of *good*?" In other words, while some of us are less likely than others to become terrorists, in the mirror of God's law we are all wicked. We all fail to love God and our neighbor in countless ways every day. So the real question is, "Why does the world include *any* good?" Apart from God's providence, September 11 would have been a normal day. Yet we all know that it was, in fact, abnormal. Even though such terrorism is an ever-present threat, God's common grace usually restrains it from happening. Because of the depravity of the human heart and the corruption of institutions in which sinful habits have become deeply embedded, things are often bad, but they are never as bad as they could be, thanks to God's common grace. In his common, although not saving, mercy, God placed a "mark" on violent Cain, and so even he was able to build a city (see Genesis 4:15, 17).

Second, through his common grace God restrains his own just wrath. Because of this grace, God was "longsuffering" in the face of human depravity "in the days of Noah" (1 Peter 3:20 NKJV). Then, after the flood, God covenanted with us and all living creatures never to destroy the earth again by water (Genesis 9:8–17). Again (although this *overlaps* in time and space with God's plan to save his people), God's common grace led him to overlook human ignorance before Christ (see Acts 17:30) and now leads him to delay his final judgment (see Romans 2:4; 2 Peter 3:9).

Common grace not only mercifully restrains sin and wrath, but, third, it is also the means by which God gives us much tangible good. Murray writes,

[God] not only restrains evil in men but he also endows men with gifts, talents, and aptitudes; he stimulates them with interest and purpose to the practice of virtues, the pursuance of worthy tasks, and the cultivation of arts and sciences that occupy the time, activity, and energy of men and that make for the benefit and civilization of the human race. He ordains institutions for the protection and promotion of right, the preservation of liberty, the advance of knowledge, and the improvement of physical and moral conditions.[6]

Scripture is full of examples of God's providential goodness, particularly in the Psalms. "The LORD is good to all, and his mercy is over all that he has made.... You open your hand; you satisfy the desire of every living thing" (Psalm 145:9, 16).

Some Christians think regeneration confers special benefits that render believers superior artists, politicians, businesspeople, and even parents. But both these Scriptures and experience confirm that unbelievers may excel in their vocations, and believers may fail in theirs. In the field of common endeavor ruled by God's creation and providence, there is no difference in principle between believers and unbelievers in terms of gifts and abilities.

Jesus calls on his followers to pray for their enemies for just this reason: "For he makes his sun rise on the evil and on the good, and sends rain on the just and on the unjust" (Matthew 5:45). Christians are supposed to imitate this divine attitude. In fact, it is clear from the parable of the sower (Matthew 13:1–9) that unbelievers even benefit from the Spirit's work through the Word; and it is undeniably true that although much harm has been done in the name of "Christendom," innumerable benefits have come to civilization as a result of biblical influences. When we see non-Christians, even those in nations hostile to the Christian message, showing signs of hospitality, kindness, justice, and compassion and creating great works of art, literature, and science, we do not conclude that all people are basically good after all. Rather, we conclude that God remains faithful to creation despite our unfaithfulness, and that the image of God is still preserved by God's Spirit despite human attempts to eradicate it.

Common grace benefits fallen humanity in terms of this age but does not bring about the age to come, that is, the kingdom of God. It does not save evildoers from the coming judgment, nor does it redeem art, culture, the state, or families. Unlike saving grace, it is restricted to this world before the last judgment and will not stay God's hand of justice on that dreadful day.

But this reality does not mean that it is *at odds with* saving grace. As John Murray says, "Special grace does not annihilate but rather brings its redemptive, regenerative, and sanctifying influence to bear on every natural or common gift; it transforms all activities and departments of life; it brings every good gift into the service of the kingdom of God. Christianity is not a flight from nature; it is the renewal and sanctification of nature." He rightly observes that this perspective challenges ascetic and monastic versions of spirituality because "its practical outlook has been, 'For every creature of God is good, and nothing [is] to be refused, if it be received with thanksgiving: for it is sanctified by the word of God and prayer' (1 Timothy 4:4, 5)."[7]

When we, as Christians, affirm common grace, we take this world seriously, in all of its sinfulness as well as in all of its goodness, as created and sustained by God. We see Christ as the mediator of saving grace to the elect but also of God's general blessings to a world that is under the curse. This allows us to participate in secular culture, to enjoy relationships with unbelievers, and to work beside them in common vocations and toward common goals without always having to justify such cooperation and common life in terms of ministry and outreach. For me, this has been one of the most liberating and practical aspects of scriptural teaching, but one that is often undervalued even in our own circles, where believers are regularly expected to justify their existence by pursuing some ministry in the church rather than by pursuing their secular callings.

Not only can unbelievers, by common grace, sustain their own goods, truths, and beauties; they can also enrich believers' lives. This is because the Father's designs, the mediation of Christ, and the power of the life-giving Spirit are no less vital to the sustaining of the world in its fallenness than they are to the redemption of sinners and the renewal of the creation at the end of history. It helps us to appreciate the depth not only of human depravity but also of human dignity because of an awareness of God's creation and common grace. In a celebrated passage, John Calvin pleads against the fanaticism that would forbid all secular influence on Christians, concluding that when we disparage the truth, goodness, and beauty found among unbelievers, we are heaping contempt on the Holy Spirit himself:

> Whenever we come upon these matters in secular writers, let that admirable light of truth shining in them teach us that the mind of man, though fallen and perverted from its wholeness, is nevertheless clothed and ornamented with God's excellent gifts. If we regard the Spirit of God as the sole fountain of truth, we shall neither reject the truth itself, nor despise it wherever it shall appear, unless we wish to dishonor the Spirit of God. For by holding the gifts of the Spirit in slight esteem, we condemn and reproach the Spirit himself. What then? Shall we deny that the truth shone upon the ancient jurists who established civic order and discipline with such great equity? Shall we say that the philosophers were blind in their fine observation and

artful description of nature? Shall we say that those men were devoid of understanding who conceived the art of disputation and taught us to speak reasonably? Shall we say that they are insane who developed medicine, devoting their labor to our benefit? What shall we say of all the mathematical sciences? Shall we consider them the ravings of madmen? No, we cannot read the writings of the ancients on these subjects without great admiration.... But shall we count anything praiseworthy or noble without recognizing at the same time that it comes from God?... Those men whom Scripture calls "natural men" were, indeed, sharp and penetrating in their investigation of inferior things. Let us, accordingly, learn by their example how many gifts the Lord left to human nature even after it was despoiled of its true good.[8]

Elsewhere, Calvin even quotes pagan poets and philosophers on religious topics—a practice sanctioned by the apostle Paul's example in Acts 17. To be sure, with Scripture as our "spectacles" through which to see reality, even the matters we commonly regard as "secular" take on a new slant. God's wisdom reorients us to see everything differently. And yet, God's goodness and wisdom are not absent even from those who willingly refuse to acknowledge his revealed Word.

Even pagan rulers exercise their dominion as a result of God's providence (Romans 13:1–7; 1 Peter 2:14)—and here Paul and Peter have in mind a government hostile to the cause of Christ. Yet even through these powers God secretly governs the nations, just as he does his church. To believe that a government must be framed according to "the political system of Moses" rather than according to "the common laws of nations," Calvin wrote, "is perilous and seditious" as well as "false and foolish."[9] The Mosaic theocracy was limited to the old covenant and is no longer the blueprint at a time when there is no chosen nation. The law of God written upon the conscience of every person allows for a marvelous diversity in constitutions, forms of government, and laws, all of which are in their own times and places acceptable as long as they preserve the "equity ... [that] must be the goal and rule and limit of all laws."[10]

Understanding this distinction helps us to recognize God's involvement in everything—the common as well as the holy, providence as well as miracle—so that we do not have to find a "spiritual" interpretation for every event. Further, we can make full use of natural explanations without trying to figure out what God might be doing behind the scenes.

God's Direct and Indirect Government

The example of Joseph telling his brothers concerning their past treachery, "You meant evil against me, but God meant it for good" (Genesis 50:20) is paradigmatic of the distinction we are considering here. So, too, is Acts 2, where Peter places the blame for Jesus' death squarely on the shoulders of those people who took part in his crucifixion and yet also affirms that Jesus was delivered up according to God's foreordination and plan. Just as God rules the affairs of his creation no less through providence than miracle, or common grace than saving grace, he is just as active when he works through creatures as when he directly brings about his designs apart from them.

If Scripture holds humans responsible for their own actions and yet affirms God's sovereignty, so too must we. These two truths are never resolved in Scripture, but held together, acknowledging their mystery. In a recent interview, the sister of a prominent victim of a savage murder said that of all those she had blamed most, God headed the list—until, that is, a wise pastor told her this was not an act of God but an act of human cruelty. That pastor was right. While God was directly involved in the death of his Son, he was not directly involved in the murder of this woman's sister. Although God is sovereign over all events, and so can always bring an ultimate good out of evil, he is not the assailant. And because he is Lord of all, he both restrains the damage that evil can cause and remembers it for the day of judgment.

Ironically, many today who would not affirm a classic Christian notion of divine sovereignty will nevertheless often speak as if God does all things in their lives directly and immediately, without any instrumental means. If someone attributes a remarkable recovery from an illness to the skill of physicians, well-meaning Christians often reply, "Yes, but God was the one who healed her." Sometimes believers even excuse their laziness and lack of wisdom or preparation by appealing to God's sovereignty: "Just pray about it," or, "Well, if God wants it to happen, it will happen," and so forth.

Granted, belief in God's providence should assure us that ultimately our times are in his hands; but God does not fulfill all of his purposes directly and immediately. Ordinarily, he employs *means*, whether people, weather patterns, social upheavals, animal migrations, various vocations, or a host of other factors over which he has ultimate control. He even used secular treaty patterns of political organization to institute his covenantal relationship with his people.

Calvin calls God's providence "the determinative principle of all things," even though "sometimes it works through an intermediary, sometimes without an intermediary, sometimes contrary to every intermediary."[11] This is the careful nuance that is often missing in debates today, in which it is supposed that God either does not rule over all or rules over all in such a way as to dispense with creaturely freedom. Calvin compares what God decrees in his hidden will to a "deep abyss," in contrast to what God has "set forth familiarly" in his revealed will:

And it is, indeed, true that in the law and the gospel are comprehended mysteries which tower far above the reach of our senses. But since God illumines the minds of his own with the spirit of discernment for the understanding of these mysteries which he has deigned to reveal by his Word, now no abyss is here; rather, a way in which we ought to walk in safety, and a lamp to guide our feet, the light of life, and the school of sure and clear truth. *Yet his wonderful method of governing the universe is rightly called an abyss, because while it is hidden from us, we ought reverently to adore it.*[12] (emphasis added).

At the same time, Calvin affirms that we can know much about how the universe operates through studying the secondary causes by which God brings his hidden will to pass; and so he rebukes anyone who would use the doctrine of God's providence as an excuse for fatalism: "For he who has set the limits to our life has at the same time entrusted to us its care; he has provided means and helps to preserve it; he has also made us able to foresee dangers; that they may not overwhelm us unaware, he has offered precautions and remedies."[13] We are, therefore, obligated to study these secondary causes so we can appropriate them. No doubt God has planned our future and is actively bringing it to pass. Yet, "nevertheless, a godly man will not overlook the secondary causes."[14]

If someone has cancer, he or she should not wait for God to miraculously intervene, but go to the best cancer clinic possible. If one's children are not following the Lord, one should not simply wait for God to bring them to their senses, but pray and ask God to bring friends and coworkers into their lives to bring them around. If we are puzzling over whom we should marry or where we should live, we should not wait around for a sign, but ask God for wisdom and make informed decisions.

When we find our marriage on the rocks, instead of playing the victim and wondering why God has allowed this to happen, we have to take stock of the secondary causes. We need to seek good counsel, surround ourselves with godly fellowship, renew our vows in tangible ways by attacking our own selfishness, share in daily prayer and Scripture reading, and, above all, make use of the means of grace—Word and Sacrament together in public worship.

So we can say, without any injury to piety, that the doctors healed us from a particular illness *and* God healed us, just as we can thank God and the baker for our daily bread. When a natural disaster strikes, our fate is not ultimately in the hands of the Federal Emergency Management Agency (FEMA), but this does not mean that God will not get us back on our feet through this government service. This perspective opens up our horizon to see God at work in all of life, even where we do not usually expect to find him, and to trust that even when we do not find him, he is already there.

I am not for one moment denying that miracles do indeed occur in people's lives. But what shall we say of the countless cases of documented recovery that were produced by human ingenuity and medical technology? Why must we call the birth of a child—probably the most spectacular example of ordinary divine providence—"a miracle," in order to acknowledge God as its ultimate source? A child's birth is clearly *not* a miracle; it does not result from God directly and immediately intervening in the natural course of things. It is the ordinary result of the right use of the proper means, from conception to delivery. Nothing could be more natural. And yet nothing could be a more marvelous testimony to God's providence.

Christians must recognize God's hand not only in the marvel of miracle but also in the splendor of providence. Here, once more, Calvin's previously noted insights are helpful: "Nothing is more natural than for spring to follow winter; summer, spring; and fall, summer, each in turn," he writes. "Yet in this series one sees such great and uneven diversity that it readily appears each year, month, and day is governed by a new, a special, providence of God."[15] Naturalistic deism, which sees nature as a great cosmic machine obeying rigid and inviolable laws, simply cannot account for the diversity that both our experience and the natural sciences betray. This is one reason why the rigid Newtonian picture has been rejected by contemporary science, just as we must reject it on the basis of Scripture. But hyper-supernaturalism comes no closer to bringing us confidence that God is at work even when and where we least expect him.

Providence and the Cross

Throughout this book, we are viewing suffering through the lens of the cross and the resurrection, so we should conclude this chapter with a brief comment in relation to providence. God's watchful care over the planets, the tides, the falling of a bird, and the rising of an empire takes place this side of Eden. That is why we call it common *grace*. Grace is a post-fall phenomenon. The world, including humanity, was created in integrity. But God's grace and mercy are shown to a world in sin. God's providence after the fall corresponds to the cross.

As we see in Colossians, Christ is the center not only of redemption but of creation ("all things were created by him and for him," 1:16 NIV) and providence as well ("and in him all things hold together," verse 17 NIV). What's more, his rule in providence is made to serve his rule in redemption, so that all of human history is made to serve, in ways hidden to us, the gathering of his people: "And he is the head of the body, the church.... For in him all the fullness of God was pleased to dwell, and through him to reconcile to himself all things, whether on earth or in heaven, making peace by the blood of the cross" (verses

18 – 20). Paul adds, "For in him the whole fullness of deity dwells bodily, and you have been filled in him, who is the head of all rule and authority" (2:9 – 10). Even now, Christ is ruling the world in providence in the service of creating his church in all ages. No wonder all things work together for good for God's people!

Just as at the cross God's power is hidden in weakness and his wisdom in folly, the world cannot see God's power and wisdom in the circumstances of this world, with all of the 9/11s, AIDS, cancer, hurricanes, and countless personal tragedies we all encounter. God's providence cannot really be discerned apart from the gospel, apart from the knowledge that God is up to something here that will turn Good Friday into Easter morning. Just as the dejected disciples could not see anything in Christ's suffering but the ultimate tragedy, we cannot turn on the news and conclude that all is right with the world. So it is to the resurrection that we now turn.

part two:
GOD of the
empty tomb

chapter seven
out of the whirlwind

Even now my witness is in heaven;
my advocate is on high.
My intercessor is my friend
as my eyes pour out tears to God;
on behalf of a human being he pleads with God
as one pleads for a friend.

Job 16:19 – 21 TNIV

I know that my Redeemer lives,
and that in the end he will stand upon the earth.
And after my skin has been destroyed,
yet in my flesh I will see God;
I myself will see him
with my own eyes — I, and not another.
How my heart yearns within me!

Job 19:25 – 27 NIV

We keep returning to the story of Job because it never fails to scratch where we itch when trials overwhelm us. I was drawn to Job in a fresh way some years ago after a close friend and fellow pastor took his life. For the purpose of our story, I'll call him Steve.

He and his amazing wife had come through intensely trying medical problems with their own children. A year or so after climbing the Matterhorn, this avid outdoorsman was struck by a train while trying to find his way out of a thick forest in the Rockies. Both legs had to be amputated. Thereafter, Steve suffered from phantom pain, his neurological system acting as if he were still experiencing the accident. It took a lot of prescription drugs just to give Steve a few hours of sleep each night.

Although we had established a friendship in California, he had moved east, and I had been pretty lax about keeping in touch. At many times during Steve's crisis, I should have been more involved. I now know that at least part of my reticence was due to the grotesque nature of what he had become—which is a terrible thing to say, of course. Steve had been a successful, athletic, world-embracing guy, and now he was in perpetual anguish. I had seen this phenomenon firsthand while growing up in my parents' rest home, as children in some cases practically abandoned their parents because they could not face their own mortality.

We live in that sort of culture, where, despite the quantum leaps in medical technology toward extending life, people who are old or terminally ill or disabled (mentally or physically) often suffer lonely lives. We are scandalized by the fragility of our own health. Even as Christians, we sometimes think of sickness, disease, and death as random events that have no meaning and must therefore be cured, at whatever cost. Sometimes we forget the connection between the fall—sin as part of the human condition—and physical and mental health.

We daily face the reality that we are who we are now, and in the next moment we could be someone else. A young professional full of promise and well on the way to becoming a partner at the law firm is the victim of a hit-and-run while jogging after work. A mother pouring her life into caring for a thriving brood is told she has terminal cancer. After two decades of what seems like an exemplary marriage, a husband wakes up to find his wife has left him and the children for another man. These were all cases I had confronted in my own ministry—and now here was a fellow pastor who had brought tragedy entirely too close for comfort.

In any case, weary from who knows how many sleepless nights, agonizing over his burdens on a family already stressed by a severely autistic little girl, and barely alert as a result of various medications, Steve went into the garage and ended his life by carbon monoxide poisoning. His wife asked me to preach at his memorial service.

Steve was a well-known pastor of a highly respected center-city church, and it seemed that everybody had a theological opinion about why he had done it and where he would end up as a result. A few commented to the press that in their understanding of suicide, Steve would be eternally condemned. In the midst of all this chatter, Job's story came to mind, and it was the story I told in the sermon on that confusing day.

Suicide is the ultimate act of despair. We find ourselves filled with a variety of emotions—pity, sorrow, rage, puzzlement, resentment—and we wonder how things could possibly have ended this way. We wonder how someone who believed and preached the sufficiency of God's Word and his grace in the face of all trials of life could leave us on a summer afternoon. "If it was not sufficient for him," we wonder, "is it indeed sufficient for me? What happens when Christianity doesn't work?"

Our culture has come to value only things that are practical, things that work. Every idea or conviction is judged by its utility: *Will it help me raise my kids, build a successful marriage, live a healthy life?* When an idea or conviction doesn't come through, we find it easy to move on to another product. So often, when people come to Christ, they are promised "victory in Jesus." Smiling people tell about how they once were unhappy, but now they are filled with buoyant exultation. Broken marriages are fixed, wayward children are returned to the straight and narrow, and depression is banished.

But, of course, naive triumphalism was not Steve's message. He did not see Christianity as the solution to every earthly problem, nor did he worship Jesus as Mr. Fix-It, but as the Friend of sinners, Redeemer, and Shepherd of his sheep. He knew there was a greater problem that we as fallen creatures face. He did not dismiss earthly challenges as irrelevant or trivial; he placed them in their proper eternal perspective. Even if life falls apart, God remains God, his purposes cannot fail, and he has proved this by raising his Son from the dead. Even if Christianity does not answer every problem we have in this life, surely the eternal perspective helps us cope with them.

"So why," we wondered, "did our father, brother, husband, friend, and pastor cut his life short?"

An Ancient Drama

Job was a man deeply devoted to God. So zealous was he for his family that whenever they left after the many homecomings they enjoyed, Job would offer a sacrifice on behalf of his children on their journey. Satan chided God for Job's faithfulness. "Why wouldn't he be faithful?" Satan asked. After all, he lived a charmed life. He was happy, wealthy, and wise, his household was carefree — the ideal family on a Norman Rockwell postcard. So God allowed Satan to test Job. There's no getting around the facts of the case: God not only *foreknew* Satan's testing, he *sanctioned* it (Job 1:6 – 12). It is clear from the story that Satan could not have had access to Job apart from God's permission.

The next day, disaster followed disaster, and overnight Job lost nearly everything precious to him. Yet Job responded,

"Naked I came from my mother's womb, and naked I will depart. The LORD gave and the LORD has taken away; may the name of the LORD be praised" (1:21 NIV). Job refused to charge God with wrongdoing.

Satan came to God again and taunted, "But stretch out your hand and strike his flesh and bones, and he will surely curse you to your face" (2:5 NIV). Job's body became racked with sores and pain until his own wife begged, "Curse God and die!" But Job still replied, "Shall we accept good from God, and not trouble?" (2:9–10 NIV).

At this point, in walk Job's famous counselors. At first they respond well, spending a week simply sitting with him, refusing to say anything because they see his pain. What he needs is friendship, not a flow of lectures. They listen to his cry of despair as he curses the day of his birth. A deep, dark cloud of depression has fallen over Job, and he can only wish he had never been born.

But then they begin to express their opinions about what is going on in Job's life. Eliphaz leads off by telling him, "Think how you have instructed many, how you have strengthened feeble hands. Your words have supported those who stumbled; you have strengthened faltering knees. But now trouble comes to you, and you are discouraged; it strikes you, and you are dismayed. Should not your piety be your confidence and your blameless ways your hope?" (4:3–6 NIV). This is the religion of the natural man or woman. By nature, we believe we are basically good people who occasionally do rotten things. In the end, the good outweighs the bad, and people get what's coming to them. This is how our natural reason assesses things. A few years back, Rabbi Harold Kushner, after losing his son, wrote *When Bad Things Happen to Good People*, the assumption being that most of us deserve better than we get because we are basically good.

Eliphaz adds, "Consider now: Who, being innocent, has ever perished? Where were the upright ever destroyed? As I have observed, those who plow evil and those who sow trouble reap it" (4:7–8 NIV). This too just makes sense: "Good guys finish first." "Cheaters never prosper."

Eliphaz is quick to return to his baseline theology, encouraging Job to accept God's discipline with the confidence that it will all work out well, as it always does if people just trust and obey (5:17–27). The riches will be restored, health will return, and Job and his friends will laugh about it in years to come. Answers come easily, too easily, for many of us at a time like this.

Job's reply is honest: "What prospects [do I have], that I should be patient? Do I have the strength of stone? Is my flesh bronze?" (6:11–12 NIV). How can he keep from presenting his complaint to the highest court? "Therefore I will not restrain my mouth; I will speak in the anguish of my spirit; I will complain in the bitterness of my soul" (7:11). This is no stiff-upper-lip approach to suffering. It is a courtroom scene, and Job will have his case heard. Like the rest of us, Job expresses his frustration at his situation, which actually begins to open him up to serious wrestling with God.

Job loathes his once-sturdy body, now plagued with disease: "I prefer strangling and death, rather than this body of mine," he cries (7:15 NIV). Turning to God, Job begs for answers: "Will you never look away from me, or let me alone even for an instant? If I have sinned, what have I done to you, O watcher of men? Why have you made me your target? Have I become a burden to you? Why do you not pardon my offenses and forgive my sins?" (7:19–21 NIV). The natural assumption in the face of such suffering is that somehow God is punishing us for our sins. But we readers of the book of Job, in the audience of this play, know from the prologue that this test had another source. Like Job, we make conclusions based on limited information, trying to figure out why things are happening to us. We don't have access to God's filing cabinet, to his inner chamber, and he does not directly tell us why bad things are happening. But this doesn't keep us from drawing conclusions anyway. Whereas we often ask in times of distress where God is and why he has hidden his face from us, Job's despair poses the opposite problem: When will God look *away* from him and move on to punish someone else?

Enter Bildad the Shuhite. Repeating the same errors as Eliphaz, Bildad cautions Job to refrain from such despair. "If you are pure and upright, and plead with the Lord, he will make everything better," he tells his suffering friend (8:5–6, my paraphrase). "Your beginnings will seem humble, so prosperous will your future be," he promises, like a modern-day TV evangelist (8:7 NIV). Bildad means well, but he too suffers from bad theology.

Once more, Job replies with sound doctrine: "But how can a mortal be righteous before God?" (9:1 NIV). God doesn't bargain with us, Job retorts, as if to say that if we do our best, he will make our life prosperous. Job declares, in effect, "Who can reply to God?" God is sovereign, "wise in heart and mighty in strength" (9:4), ruling over the planets and stars as well as the affairs of mortals (9:4–14). At this point, though, Job still shares the baseline theology of his friends but protests his personal innocence: "Though I am in the right, I cannot answer him; I must appeal for mercy to my accuser" (9:15).

It is clear from the following verses that Job is willing to throw himself on the mercy of the court only reluctantly—because he can never win: "If it is a contest of strength, behold, he is mighty! If it is a matter of justice, who can summon him?" (9:19). He begins to realize that he shares with the rest of humanity a depravity that only shows up on the radar when compared to God. Standing in a lineup with other mortals,

Job appears innocent. But compared to God, "my own mouth would condemn me; though I am blameless, he would prove me perverse" (9:20). "I become afraid of all my suffering, for I know you will not hold me innocent. I shall be condemned; why then do I labor in vain? If I wash myself with snow and cleanse my hands with lye, yet you will plunge me into a pit, and my own clothes will abhor me. For he is not a man, as I am, that I might answer him, that we should come to trial together" (9:28–32).

Here the horns of the dilemma well established in the historic problem-of-evil debate are captured in a terse summary: whatever the answer to our grief, God is sovereign and just. Easy answers will sacrifice one for the other: either God is all-powerful or good, but he cannot be both. Job refuses to justify himself at God's expense, at least for now. Job concludes that if God destroyed both the pious and the wicked alike, he would be justified in his actions, for no one is righteous. Bad things happen to bad people, good things happen to bad people, but there is no such thing as bad things happening to good people. There is no one good, no not one.

Needed: A Good Attorney

Even though Job insists he has done nothing to warrant God's direct punishment in this particular crisis (and he is correct here), he recognizes that he cannot appeal to his own righteousness. And just at this point, Job realizes what he lacks if he is going to appear in court with God: a good lawyer, a defense attorney, a mediator. "There is no arbiter between us, who might lay his hand on us both" and remove the heavy rod. If only there were such a mediator. "Then I would speak without fear of him, for I am not so in myself" (9:33, 35). Do we grasp the distance between this God-centered approach to suffering and human-centered ones? Even the bad theologians that Job had counted as friends were talking about Job's case in terms of sin and justice, which leads to Job's cry for a mediator. The courtroom is the dominant atmosphere, with God as the judge (and also, in a sense, on trial). If we fail to see the connection between sin and suffering (even if we rightly avoid attributing specific trials to specific punishments for specific sins), we never get around to asking for a good lawyer to mediate the dispute.

Seeing no mediator step forward, Job begs God, "Are not my days few? Then cease, and leave me alone, that I may find a little cheer" (10:20). How many people today turn their back on God because of a seismic calamity in their life? God's face is not a cheery smile but an ominous threat to them. It is normal in such trials even for God's children to want to turn away from God, like a steelworker turning for a moment from the blast of the furnace. If God were a good God and all-powerful, surely he could stop my suffering in one moment, we reason.

For Job, this theological question is settled. But God's sovereignty and justice cannot provide sufficient solace. Only in God's *mercy* can Job find comfort—if only he had a go-between. After all, common sense would lead a person to conclude that if God were both sovereign and just, such extraordinary disaster must be a sign of God's displeasure. This is why he cries out for some kind of defense attorney, someone to intervene, to plead his case before the judge. If he had that, Job says, he could turn to God. He could embrace him in the midst of this suffering. But as it stands, he cannot, and he wishes that God himself would turn away from him. God may indeed be justified in his ways: both almighty and just. "God's in charge" and "God is good" have their proper place in answering the crisis, but by themselves—apart from someone to mediate between the God of blinding glory and a miserable sinner—these assurances merely pour salt on the wound. They cannot, on their own, turn Job's misery to praise. In fact, if anything, such assurances are merely slogans, serving to make Job more miserable.

Zophar steps up to the plate to offer his advice. He begins, "Are all these words [of Job] to go unanswered? Is this talker to be vindicated? . . . Will no one rebuke you when you mock?" (11:2 – 3 NIV). But, of course, Job is not mocking. He is telling the truth about his situation, something that pious folks are sometimes prone to mistake for mocking.

Basically, Zophar tells Job to repent. God doesn't punish unjustly, so stop hiding your sin. Cough it up, Job. Give up that secret sin in your life. "Surely then you will lift up your face without blemish; you will be secure and will not fear. You will forget your misery; you will remember it as waters that have passed away. And your life will be brighter than the noonday; its darkness will be like the morning" (11:15 – 17).

It must be said that this is exactly the sort of platitudinous moralism one often finds in some Christian circles these days. But it is as old as the fall of humanity in the Garden of Eden. We dress ourselves with fig leaves, believing that our shame is covered by the shelter of our own righteousness. Platitudes for better living are offered instead of promises of God's unmerited favor, and Job's response is understandably as sarcastic toward his counselors as it is reverent and trusting toward God:

> Doubtless you are the people,
> and wisdom will die with you!
> But I have a mind as well as you;
> I am not inferior to you.
> Who does not know all these things?
>
> Job 12:2 – 3 NIV

> But I would speak to the Almighty,
> and I desire to argue my case with God.
> As for you, you whitewash with lies;

> *worthless physicians are you all!*
> *Oh that you would keep silent,*
> *and it would be your wisdom!...*
> *Will you speak falsely for God*
> *and speak deceitfully for him?...*
> *Will you plead the case for God?*
> *Will it be well with you when he searches you out?*
> *Or can you deceive him, as one deceives a man?...*
> *Will not his majesty terrify you,*
> *and the dread of him fall upon you?*
> *Your maxims are proverbs of ashes;*
> *your defenses are defenses of clay.*
> *Let me have silence, and I will speak,*
> *and let come on me what may....*
> *Though he slay me, I will hope in him;*
> *yet I will argue my ways to his face.*
>
> Job 13:3 – 5, 7 – 9, 11 – 13, 15

Contrary to the appraisal of his counselors, Job displays remarkable piety in the midst of this trial. It is not stoicism but an unflinching confidence in God *for his own sake*. His soul is ruled by the cry *soli Deo gloria* — to God alone be glory.

Nevertheless, Job is overwhelmed with grief and pain. He doesn't hold God's glory hostage to his own crisis, and yet he cannot help but shield his face from that glory, which can only seem oppressive to him in his weakness. When he lays out these complaints to God, Eliphaz launches another sermon: "You even undermine piety," he tells Job, "and hinder devotion to God" (15:4 NIV). Job replies, "I have heard many things like these; miserable comforters are you all! Will your long-winded speeches never end?" (16:2 – 3 NIV). More important, Job does not know what to make of God's comfort in his suffering: "Surely now God has worn me out" — stripping him even of human consolation (16:7).

And yet, in the midst of his pain, Job once again searches for a go-between, someone who can mediate this dispute and cause God to relent. "Even now, behold"—and here "behold" powerfully announces the arrival of a new character in the unfolding courtroom drama—"my witness is in heaven, and he who testifies for me is on high. My friends scorn me; my eye pours out tears to God, that he would argue the case of a man with God, as a son of man does with his neighbor" (16:19–21). Job appeals to an intercessor who is no less than God himself, yet who will plead his case "as a son of man does with his neighbor."

Even as he pours out his lament for his earthly torment, Job is able to find his way to the window, where he spies his hope. It is not the sight of renewed health, recovered wealth, or rediscovered happiness, but rather the sight of something altogether more precious in the midst of his suffering: "I know that my Redeemer lives, and that in the end he will stand upon the earth. And after my skin has been destroyed, yet in my flesh I will see God; I myself will see him with my own eyes—I, and not another. How my heart yearns within me!" (19:25–27 NIV). In addition to the remarkably clear references to a mediator in heaven who will one day stand upon the earth, what is striking here is that Job's hope for the future is *not* the liberation of his soul from his body.

Though tormented by his physical condition, his confidence is that in this same decrepit flesh he will see God. It is reference to the mediator that introduces the only notes of hope into an otherwise bleak story. We are reminded of Ephesians 2:1–5 (NKJV), which begins with the bad news that we are all "dead in trespasses and sins," "by nature children of wrath." Then there is the transition "but God, who is rich in mercy ..." It is that "but God ..." that always makes the difference, especially when it is linked specifically to God's mercy. Job is comforted not by platitudes that pretend to know God and the way the world works so well, or by abstract appeals to God's justice and sovereignty, but by the concrete hope of Easter after Good Friday.

Undaunted by Job's rebukes, the friends continue their prosecution. The young Elihu "became very angry with Job for justifying himself rather than God. He was also angry with the three friends, because they had found no way to refute Job, and yet had condemned him" (32:2–3 NIV). This man challenges the apparent self-justification. Although Job proclaims God's sovereignty and justice, his speeches are so determined to clear him of any guilt that God's sovereignty is reduced to brute force and God's justice to mere whim. Elihu's lengthy speech reasserts both (Job 32–37). He chides Job for saying that although he is in the right, God will not hear his case. It belongs to all of us to suffer as part of our common curse, he tells Job. And yet,

> *If there be for him an angel,*
> > *a mediator, one of the thousand,*
> > *to declare to man what is right for him,*
> *and he is merciful to him, and says,*
> > *"Deliver him from going down into the pit;*
> > *I have found a ransom;*
> *let his flesh become fresh with youth;*
> > *let him return to the days of his youthful vigor";*
> *then man prays to God, and he accepts him;*
> > *he sees his face with a shout of joy,*
> *and he restores to man his righteousness.*
> > *He sings before men and says:*
> *"I sinned and perverted what was right,*
> > *and it was not repaid to me.*
> *He has redeemed my soul from going down into the pit,*
> > *and my life shall look upon the light."*

Job 33:23–28

Elihu rightly points out that all along Job has not been either patient or consistent in upholding both God's majestic sovereignty and his just goodness. Although God was not punishing Job for a specific sin, suffering is part of our lot as fallen sinners. No one can say, "I am innocent. I should not be going through this." This is why we need to turn from trusting in our own righteousness to the mediator who announces to the court that he has found a ransom to deliver us from final destruction.

Only this, and not the inspirational platitudes, can truly lift one's countenance. What Job should be saying, according to Elihu, is, "I sinned and perverted what was right, and it was not repaid to me. He has redeemed my soul from going down into the pit, and my life shall look upon the light" (33:27–28). Job had struggled toward this in his previous confession of faith in a living Redeemer who will raise him from the dead, but Elihu presses him toward the place where he will stop justifying himself and accept his place with the rest of us as sinners who have no plea but Christ. Much of what God says for himself later substantiates Elihu's comments.

The Voice from Above

After Job and the friends finish their sermons, God finally speaks up and preaches for himself. Out of the whirlwind, he answers Job: "Who is this that darkens my counsel with words without knowledge? Brace yourself like a man; I will question you, and you shall answer me. Where were you when I laid the earth's foundation? Tell me, if you understand" (38:2–4 NIV). After listing a litany of divine actions that illustrate his wisdom and power over the universe, God shuts the mouths of Job and his well-meaning friends. For they have all been arguing on the basis of their own experience and common sense. They have all operated under the assumption that they could read God's mind on the surface of the events.

How easily we attempt this when suffering strikes us or our loved ones! We immediately strike out to rationalize the purpose behind it all. But God refuses to be figured out in these matters, and his counsel is hidden to mortals. God asks them all, "Can you make a pet of [me] like a bird or put [me] on a leash for your girls? ... Any hope of subduing [me] is false; the mere sight of [me] is overpowering. ... Who then is able to stand against me? Who has a claim against me that I must pay? Everything under heaven belongs to me" (41:5, 9–11 NIV).

After God's defense, Job is left without excuse. God reminds him, as he reminds all of us, that just because we don't have the answers does not mean there are no answers. Job's friends had all the answers: Job's suffering was the effect of his sin, or of his failure to claim victory over his circumstances. Refusing to buy into their works-righteousness and hollow platitudes, Job became an existentialist, preferring no answers to wrong answers. God was sovereign and just, but in the abstract, he concluded. In his concrete experience, God was someone to be shunned. Much like Jean-Paul Sartre, after the despair of two savage world wars, Job concluded that suicide might be preferable to enduring his suffering. Again and again, he has cried out to God for an end to his life.

For those who are tied to the high masts of suffering, there is often a fear greater than the fear of death. It is the fear of life. It is the fear of the next morning, and the morning after that. In the face of deep despair, the temptation is great to turn away from God because the suffering is somehow credited to his wrath toward personal sins rather than to turn toward him because one knows that he or she is at peace with God. This is why Job has said he would be able to turn toward God in this situation *if only he had a go-between, an advocate.* Gradually, he came to a greater confidence in this mediator. The confession bears repeating: "Even now my witness is in heaven; my advocate is on high. My intercessor is my friend as my eyes pour out tears to God; on behalf of a man he pleads with God as a man pleads for his friend" (16:19 – 21 NIV).

Whatever is wrong in our life, we are given an unshakable conviction that our Witness is in heaven. We know that Christ is our Intercessor, a Friend to whom we can pour out tears to God. We know that Jesus, our Elder Brother, is pleading on our behalf as a man pleads for his friend. We know the meaning of Paul's despair over his ongoing sinfulness in Romans 7, where the apostle laments, "The good that I want to do I do not do and the very thing that I do not want to do, that is what I do. . . . O wretched man that I am! Who will deliver me from this body of death?" (Romans 7:19, 24, my translation). But also like the apostle Paul, and Job, we know the answer to that question: "Thanks be to God, through our Lord Jesus Christ! . . . For there is therefore now no condemnation for those who are in Christ Jesus" (7:25 – 8:1, my translation).

So Much for Common Sense

The common sense view of things troubled the psalmist as well as Job:

> *Truly God is good to Israel,*
> *   to those who are pure in heart.*
> *But as for me, my feet had almost stumbled,*
> *   my steps had nearly slipped.*
> *For I was envious of the arrogant*
> *   when I saw the prosperity of the wicked.*
> *For they have no pangs until death;*
> *   their bodies are fat and sleek.*
> *They are not in trouble as others are;*
> *   they are not stricken like the rest of mankind.*
> *Therefore pride is their necklace;*
> *   violence covers them as a garment.*

Their eyes swell out through fatness;
their hearts overflow with follies.
They scoff and speak with malice;
loftily they threaten oppression.
They set their mouths against the heavens,
and their tongue struts through the earth.
Therefore his people turn back to them,
and find no fault in them.
And they say, "How can God know?
Is there knowledge in the Most High?"
Behold, these are the wicked;
always at ease, they increase in riches.
All in vain have I kept my heart clean
and washed my hands in innocence.
For all the day long I have been stricken
and rebuked every morning.

Psalm 73:1–14

This is the testimony of common sense, of our own experience. But the psalmist's confusion is answered by God's own wisdom:

But when I thought how to understand this,
it seemed to me a wearisome task,
until I went into the sanctuary of God;
then I discerned their end.
Truly you set them in slippery places;
you make them fall to ruin.
How they are destroyed in a moment,
swept away utterly by terrors!
Like a dream when one awakes,
O Lord, when you rouse yourself, you despise them as
phantoms.
When my soul was embittered,

when I was pricked in heart,
I was brutish and ignorant;
  I was like a beast toward you.
Nevertheless, I am continually with you;
  you hold my right hand.
You guide me with your counsel,
  and afterward you will receive me to glory.
Whom have I in heaven but you?
  And there is nothing on earth that I desire besides you.
My flesh and my heart may fail,
  but God is the strength of my heart and
    my portion forever.

Psalm 73:16–26, emphasis added

Stepping out of the darkness of God's mysterious ways in providence, the psalmist enters the sanctuary of God's revealed Word and recognizes that, although providence seems to favor the ungodly and undervalue the saints who trust in God, justice will be done at the end of it all. What happens here and now is not the whole story.

This helped me tremendously as I reflected on the inequity between the life of care that my parents gave and the peculiar type of agony that they experienced. The hand of providence is hidden to us. We really cannot read God's smile or frown from the circumstances of our life. God's paths simply cannot be sorted out. Let God be God!

Our Faith Is Not a "Fix"

Christianity is not true because it works. In many cases, it does not work. That is to say, it does not solve all the problems we think it should solve. It isn't a technique for our personal therapy, but the truth that God has overcome sin and death in the cross and resurrection of Christ. Those who became Christians because they were told it would fix their marriages, only to find themselves in divorce court, might well give up on Christianity. Those who expected to be free of all their sinful habits, temptations, and desires after a conversion in which sudden victory was promised may find themselves disillusioned with God altogether, when they realize they are still sinners saved by grace.

At that difficult funeral of a pastor, friend, father, and brother in Christ who had ended his life of suffering, many people were wondering even out loud, "If Christianity didn't work for someone like Steve, how can it work for me?" It is an honest question, an understandable question. But it assumes that Christianity fixes everything. It *doesn't* fix everything, not at least here and now. It does promise that everything will be fixed at the end of history, but in this wilderness experience, we are on pilgrimage to the Holy City. Some pilgrims will find the journey much more difficult than remaining back in Egypt, in unbelief. Steve was not one of those pilgrims who turned back to Egypt. Others will bear their lot in life as best they can, and Steve and his wife were towers of strength to me in my own pilgrimage, as I watched them meet successive disasters by turning again and again to God and his gracious promise.

But Steve was a pilgrim for whom the hike to that eternal city eventually became so heavy that he looked for a shortcut. With his godly wife, he was "longing for a better country" (Hebrews 11:16 NIV), but was unwilling to wait. He did not accept God's timing—and yet he still found a mediator who interceded for him at the Father's right hand. He, with us, will receive the prize for which he hoped, even in weakness.

We are in no better position than Job to take God to court, either for our personal trials or those we experience collectively as a people of a certain time and place; whether we are facing tragedies in our families or helplessly watching the collapse of New York's Twin Towers teeming with our fellow citizens. God did not promise any of us health, wealth, and happiness. In fact, he tells us that we who expect to share in Christ's glory will also participate in his suffering—not just suffering in general, but a special kind of trial in solidarity with Christ (Romans 8:17). The good news that we proclaim is true, not because it works for people in that pragmatic, utilitarian way, but because nearly two thousand years ago, outside of the center city of Jerusalem, the Son of God was crucified for our sins and was raised for our justification. This historical event may not fix our marriages, our relationships, or our messed-up lives the way we would like, or in the timing we would like, but it saves us from the wrath of God to come and gives us new life, hope, and wisdom for our existence here and now, guaranteeing the end of pain at last. Surely in view of this, all else pales not into insignificance but into secondary importance to that great issue: "For it is appointed for a human being once to die, and then the judgment" (Hebrews 9:27, my translation).

The perfect righteousness that God requires of us was possessed by only one human being, the Redeemer to whom Job and Paul and every other saint has looked for shelter from death and hell. The moment we trust in Jesus Christ and renounce our own claims to holiness and acceptability, stripping away the fig leaves of our own making, God clothes us in the robe of Christ's righteousness. Because of Christ's life of obedience, his sacrificial death, and his triumphant resurrection, we are accepted by the Father and made his heirs, given the Holy Spirit, and promised the resurrection of our own mortal flesh.

This means it is safe to look up to God again. As Job said that if only he had an advocate he could lift his eyes up to God in his suffering, so all of us can cry on our Father's shoulder on sorrowful afternoons, because we have nothing to fear. It is not his wrath that has sent us pain and suffering if we belong to him, for he intercepts Satan's designs and fashions even sin and evil into messengers of grace. Even if we never see this design in our own lives or in the great tragedies of history, we have confidence in God's purposes, because we do see the obvious design revealed in the greatest injustice humanity has ever perpetrated: the crucifixion of the Lord of glory. Like Job in his distress and Stephen in his martyrdom, we can face even death confidently: "Behold, I see the heavens opened, and the Son of Man standing at the right hand of God" (Acts 7:56).

Although Job rightly realized he was in no position to put God on trial, it is nevertheless the case that God himself is represented in this remarkable book as placing himself in precisely that spot. In fact, Job's trial is simply a "play within a play," a subplot within the larger plot of the cosmic trial between Satan and the triune God of history. Woven throughout all the stories in the history of Israel and its saints is the overarching plot of the two seeds: the seed of the woman and the seed of the serpent, the line of covenant promise yielding the Messiah and the "powers and principalities" of this present evil age, both struggling to bring about two antithetical plans for the world. Job's trial takes place within this larger trial in which Satan still seeks to seduce the jury into believing that God is either not good enough or powerful enough to command their homage.

Yet God triumphs because there *is* a Redeemer, a mediator, who has crushed the serpent's head and, after banishing sin and evil from his presence forever, will right all wrongs and make all things new. Our trials will never become incorporated into canonical Scripture, but they too participate in this cosmic assize, where God stoops to our level, allowing himself to be arraigned before the court of history. It is to this amazing story that we turn next.

chapter eight
a new creation

Maureen O'Hara and Walter Truett Anderson underscored over a decade ago the growing suspicion that the therapeutic industry is in bad shape. Based on her own experience as a San Diego psychotherapist, O'Hara introduces us to a few of her patients. (The names have been changed.)

Jerry feels overwhelmed, anxious, fragmented, and confused. He disagrees with people he used to agree with and aligns himself with people he used to argue with. He questions his sense of reality and frequently asks himself what it all means. He has had all kinds of therapeutic and growth experiences: Gestalt, rebirthing, Jungian analysis, holotropic breathwork, bioenergentics, "A Course in Miracles," twelve-step recovery groups, Zen meditation, Ericksonian hypnosis. He has been to sweat lodges, to the Rajneesh ashram in Poona, India, to the Wicca festival in Devon. He is in analysis again, this time with a self-psychologist. Although he is endlessly on the lookout for new ideas and experiences, he keeps saying that he wishes he could simplify his life. He talks about buying land in Oregon. He loved *Dances with Wolves*. Jerry is like so many educated professionals who come in for psychotherapy these days. But he is not quite the typical client; he is a well-established psychotherapist.[1]

Then there is Beverly, who "comes into therapy torn between two lifestyles and two identities. In the California city where she goes to college, she is a radical feminist; on visits to her Midwestern hometown, she is a nice, sweet, square, conservative girl. The therapist asks her when she feels most like herself. She says, 'When I'm on the airplane.'"

These people, O'Hara and Anderson write, "are shoppers in the great marketplace of realities that the contemporary Western world has become: here a religion, there an ideology, over there a lifestyle."[2]

Psychologist Robert Jay Lifton labels this pervasive yearning for ever-new identities "the Protean style," taken from the Greek myth in which Proteus constantly changed his shape to evade capture. Having multiple personalities used to be called a disorder, says Lifton, but it is now a common characteristic of the postmodern self.[3] I have noticed that a fashionable retail chain has been running a marketing campaign in recent years with the slogan "Reinvent Yourself." This "passion for rebirth," says Lifton, is fueled at least in part by a nagging sense of guilt that is never really confronted. Everyone wants to be someone or something else, a new creation—but on their own terms.

This cannot help but invite a vicious and ultimately unsatisfying series of rebirths precisely because they all take place, as Ecclesiastes reminds us, "under the sun" (Ecclesiastes 1:3 NIV), without any significance penetrating from outside the web of this world's everyday possibilities. "Vanity of vanities ... vanity of vanities! All is vanity," said one who had it all (1:2). Our thirst for perpetual self-transformation is largely generated by the culture of marketing. We see advertisements of people we'd like to be, having lives we'd like to live, seeing themselves and being seen in the way we'd like to see ourselves and be seen. And yet the truth is that our bodies are aging; our charisma is fading; our minds are forgetful or too often distracted by the trivial and the urgent. Our souls are so thin that we do not even know what it would be like to glorify God and enjoy him forever.

All the while, we live amidst the whirl of Vanity Fair, hoping something new will come into our lives that may change everything. We watch the fireworks, look at each other, and wonder if this is all there is to fill our lives. It is this fading age, with its false promises and money-back guarantees, makeovers, petty lust, and perpetual amusements that is in fact the "opiate of the masses," not biblical faith. Carnival numbs us to the reality of Lent, but it is Lent that leads to Easter! In other words, it is the vanity of our culture that distracts us from life in its fullness, lulling us into a childish superstition that everything is fine and the future is benign. We are like a vacant canvas, painting a different scene on ourselves in an effort not to be the person in the Beatles' song: "Nowhere man, living in his nowhere land, making all his nowhere plans for nobody."

This is not who we tend to think we are; it's not what the evangelists of cool tell us we are; but it is precisely what we know ourselves to be when the lights go on. *Nihilism* is the name we have given this phenomenon. Literally "no-thing-ism," nihilism is not resignation to one's tragic fate ("I'm a no-body"), but the heroic courage to attain mastery. There is no transcendent reference point for truth, said Nietzsche; "truth is not discovered; it is made."

At least Nietzsche's version of nihilism was rebellious. There was some life in it. Dare to be a master of the world! In the 1960s, for example, a lot of young people attempted just that, embracing Dionysian independence from all social conventions and even from claims to ultimate truth and morality. Therefore, it's probably not quite right to call Nietzsche's brand of atheism "nihilism," since his claim was not that there is *no thing* to believe in, but that if we believe in ourselves we can make truth and create reality not only for ourselves but for everyone else. The masters win.

Today, however, a lot of young people really *are* nihilists. If for Nietzsche truth was not discovered but made, for many today truth is not even made but passively worn like a dress, adopted from popular culture. Not really happy, but also not sad; not really loved, but also not deprived — in fact, pampered — a lot of us simply sit back and let the true Nietzschean masters of the previous generation entertain us, feeding us their images of the true, the good, and the beautiful. Nihilism is having two hundred TV channels from which to choose, life as a perpetual smorgasbord in which choice becomes an end in itself. We forget what we're even choosing or why. We are "in charge," but of a life that seems often to lack any definite purpose or sense of destination. So people conform their bodies to the fashion magazines, their souls to the self-help fads, and then return to suburban anonymity to start all over the next day. This restless, reckless, Dionysian pursuit of physical and spiritual "makeovers" is its own form of suffering. The masters have become slaves after all.

Into this culture of restless change leading nowhere, the gospel's light comes, proclaiming that something has happened outside us, in history — a divine disruption that really has inaugurated a new world (Revelation 21:5). The Holy Spirit has been sent by the Father and by the Son, who sits victorious at the Father's right hand, to make all things genuinely new from the inside out. Even now, the future consummation is breaking into "this present evil age" (Galatians 1:4 NASB), working like leaven in a lump of dough (see Matthew 13:33; Luke 13:21). It does not promise a better you, or a new look or style, or a new image, but a genuinely new creation.

This new creation is God's work. It is humanity's only real hope. I will here indicate in broad strokes what Paul has to say about this "new creation" in the book of Romans.

Two Adams (Romans 5:12 – 21)

After concluding in Romans 3:9 – 20 that the whole world stands condemned either by the law written on tablets (as it was for the Old Testament Jews) or by the law written on the conscience (as it is for everyone else), Paul announces God's free justification of sinners in Christ alone through faith alone by grace alone (see Romans 3:21 – 31). This leads to his opening the fifth chapter of Romans with these words: "Therefore, since we have been justified by faith, we have peace with God through our Lord Jesus Christ." Here is real peace, real rest, that is not primarily a feeling (and thus some pious goal to be strived for by super-saints) but a real change in status before God, a change in status from standing guilty before God to standing righteous before him. This status is the objective possession of even the weakest believer.

This is a crucial point, because it is especially in times of tribulation that we are least likely to have that "peaceful, easy feeling." On top of whatever difficulty we're going through, we now have the added worry that our current experience (or lack thereof) somehow demonstrates that God is not with us or on our side. Of immeasurable comfort in such circumstances is the certain knowledge that God has reconciled us to himself, regardless of what our daily spiritual temperature might be. The peace that Paul is talking about here depends on the fact that we have already been "reconciled to God by the death of his Son" (Romans 5:10), justified before God once and for all through faith in Christ's work. It will certainly generate both feelings and actions, but this peace with God that Paul describes rests securely on the work of Christ for us, outside us, in history. It is not just the *cessation of hostilities* between God and us (although it includes this), but the *presence of divine blessing* and fellowship. No subjective condition of our hearts, doubts in our minds, or affliction of our bodies will be able to change what God has already done for us once and for all in Christ.

Immediately after this declaration, Paul launches into his discussion of the two Adams and their roles as the representative heads of all humanity. Each one of us is either "in Adam" (and consequently spiritually dead; see 1 Corinthians 15:22) or "in Christ" (and consequently spiritually alive; see Romans 6:11). Moreover, our union with Adam or Christ — our being "in Adam" or "in Christ" — is both *federal* and *organic*.

By "federal" I mean representative and covenantal. Just as Thomas Jefferson spoke and acted for all Americans, born and yet unborn, when he drafted the Declaration of Independence, so God at creation appointed Adam to speak and act for the entire human race. In other words, God made Adam the legal and covenantal head of the human race. When Adam chose to disobey God, he acted not only for himself and his immediate family but also for all of his descendants, for all human beings. God's resulting legal judgment indicted the entire human race. "Through one man's offense judgment came to all men, resulting in condemnation" (Romans 5:18 NKJV).

But this union with Adam is not just a matter of law and covenantal order; it also has an organic aspect. Just as a branch of an apple tree is part of that tree and consequently shares that tree's botanical strengths and weaknesses, so we as Adam's children organically share his corruption. As his heirs, Adam's disobedience is not only legally imputed to us, but his fallenness is also organically imparted to us. And so the law's righteous demands not only go unfulfilled by the children of Adam but also are actively suppressed.

The contrast with those who are in Christ could not be greater. Paul elsewhere calls Christ the "last Adam" in order to stress that Christ (rather than the first Adam) is the representative head of all who believe (see 1 Corinthians 15:45–49). Just as his resurrection is the dawn of the future glorification of our bodies (see Romans 6:5; 1 Corinthians 15:20–22, 35–56), so Christ's vindication before the Father in his triumphant ascension secures for us our full acceptance before God (see 2 Corinthians 5:14–21; Ephesians 4:7–8): "But the free gift is not like the trespass. For if many died through one man's trespass, much more have the grace of God and the free gift by the grace of that one man Jesus Christ abounded for many" (Romans 5:15). The verdict of the last day is rendered here and now. For us, judgment day is a settled affair.

We are legally justified by virtue of Christ's perfect obedience credited to us (see also 2 Corinthians 5:21), and we are organically united to Christ in such a way that the most relevant metaphors drawn throughout the New Testament are those of a vine and its branches (see John 15:1–8), a head and the rest of the body (see Ephesians 5:23; Colossians 1:18; 2:19), the temple and its constituent "living stones" (see 1 Peter 2:4–5), and so forth. Organic imagery is selected, first of all, because it underscores the solidarity, the common life, of the head and its members. Through faith in Christ we not only inherit Christ's legal justification before the throne of God; we also become so vitally connected to him by the mysterious work of the Spirit that his very life becomes the source of transformation of our own lives (see Romans 8:9–11; Galatians 2:20). We live because he lives. We feed on Christ through Word and Sacrament, as the powers of the age to come break in on this present evil age.

The fact that our union through faith with Christ has both federal and organic aspects is extremely important. This is because we can easily separate justification and sanctification, the legal verdict and the transformed life, in a way that ends up emphasizing one to the exclusion of the other. On one hand, we can so revel in the blessing of the forgiveness of our sins and our justification before God that we neglect the reality of the new birth that converts us and "turns us around" (as the biblical words for *conversion* and *repentance* imply). On the other hand, we can be so overcome with the magnitude of our conversion that we cling to it rather than to Christ and fail to see that our sanctification, no less than our justification, has Christ as its source. Too often, "Christian life" programs separate these two aspects of our union with Christ so that believers end up living schizophrenic lives, trusting in the sufficiency of Christ for their justification and yet trying to attain victory over sin from some other source.

But there is a key difference between election, atonement, and justification on one hand (the *accomplishment* of our redemption) and the new birth, conversion, repentance, and sanctification on the other (the *application* of our redemption). Or, to put it a little differently, there is a difference between Christ's work *for* us and his work *in* us. God's electing, reconciling, and justifying work is perfect and complete. Nothing can be added to the perfect righteousness of Christ, no work left undone, no effort spared, nothing lacking that needs to be supplemented by us. In fact, to suggest that we can add anything to our redemption is to insult God's liberal expense in making us his children. We cannot be more chosen, accepted, forgiven, or justified than we are right now.

The renewal of creation, however, is a process that is incomplete in this age (on a cosmic scale) and in our own lives (on a personal scale). It begins with regeneration, the gracious work of the Spirit through the gospel, by which we are definitively, once and for all, never-to-be-undone, made new creatures in Christ, inserted into the everlasting life of the coming age. Yet we are being progressively conformed to the image of Christ. Sanctification does not happen all at once. Whatever radical conversion some of us may have had, it did not end the warfare with sin but only began it. Life is a continual battle, a daily dying to self and being raised in newness of life, a perpetual repentance in the face of failures and struggle against sin.

Our worry in our Christian experience, whether due to physical suffering or spiritual depression, has a lot to do with what we expect from this "new creation." Just how new is it? Sometimes heaven seems so close I could reach out and touch it. I feel an inner strength to battle against doubt, sin, and temptation. Then at other times I feel like I'm not making any progress at all, that I am struggling with the same issues that held me in bondage before I was born again into the new creation. Theologians often refer to this as "the already" and "the not yet," and these categories are helpful in understanding Paul's arguments in Romans 6 – 8.

"Already" (Romans 6)

What is truly marvelous about this section of Paul's famous epistle is how he links justification and sanctification in terms of our union with Christ. Corresponding to the two Adams is death in Adam and life in Christ. After observing that "where sin increased, grace abounded all the more" (Romans 5:20), Paul anticipates the logical reply: "What shall we say then? Are we to continue in sin that grace may abound?" (6:1).

These questions have gotten a lot of different answers in pastoral counseling, in sermons, and in Christian literature. Sometimes the answer seems to be, "Sure! What a great setup: God likes to forgive, and I like to sin!" Most Christians, however, reply otherwise. But how do they answer, more specifically? Sometimes with threats: "If you do continue to live in sin, you may lose your salvation," or, "you may lose your rewards," or, "you will become a carnal Christian and fail to live the victorious Christian life."

Yet notice how Paul replies: "By no means! How can we who died to sin still live in it?" (6:2). Victory over the tyranny of sin is not some goal to be attained only by super-saints but is already the present possession of every believer who has been "baptized into [Christ's] death" (6:3). In other words, every believer is a victorious Christian in terms of the gospel, but no believer is as victorious as the usual "victorious Christian" teaching implies.

But first, here in chapter 6, Paul is very explicit about the "already": "We were buried therefore with him by baptism into death, in order that, just as Christ was raised from the dead by the glory of the Father, we too might walk in newness of life" (6:4). This is his explanation as to why all believers are already definitively changed once and for all, incapable of returning to spiritual death. "We were buried therefore with him by baptism into death." For those of us who have been united with Christ through faith, being baptized into his death is—just like his own death and resurrection—a completed event, expressed in this passage by the Greek language's aorist tense. Just as we have been justified, we have been baptized. Through union with Christ, the Holy Spirit sweeps us into that future world, that resurrection world, that age defined by Christ rather than by Adam (6:5–11). It is through faith alone that we receive the new life promised and sealed to us in our baptism, but this faith itself is part of the new life that God gives. Those who are spiritually dead cannot resurrect themselves.

Paul is not issuing a command at the beginning of Romans 6; he is making an announcement! Life in Christ by the power of the Spirit is not something to be attained by us but something that has already been given to us, and this we are to recognize as already having been given to us because of our union with Christ. Baptism's decisiveness—done once, never to be repeated—assures us of the decisiveness of this act of rebirth and renewal, toppling Satan's reign in our lives. Thus, Christian warfare is waged on the basis of Christ's victory and not on the basis of our attainments. We fight from victory to victory. We can stand in the battle because the war has already been won and the enemy has already been defeated!

Elsewhere Paul writes, "Since, then, you have been raised with Christ, set your hearts on things above, where Christ is seated at the right hand of God. Set your minds on things above, not on earthly things. For you died [past tense], and your life is now [present tense] hidden with Christ in God. When Christ, who is your life, appears, then you also will appear [future tense] with him in glory" (Colossians 3:1–4 NIV). Paul then continues: "Put to death, therefore, whatever belongs to your earthly nature" (3:5 NIV). And so it is on the basis of what *God* has done, is doing, and will yet do because of our union with Christ that we obey his commands.

This is why Paul now turns in Romans 6 from the *indicative* mood (announcing what is done) to the *imperative* mood (exhorting us to act as a result): "Let not sin therefore reign in your mortal bodies, to make you obey their passions.... For sin *will have no dominion over you*, since you are not under law but under grace" (Romans 6:12, 14, emphasis added). Sin *cannot* rule those who are baptized into Christ by water and the Spirit, because in truth they have passed out of death into life (see also 1 John 3:14). In this way, God has already broken the bondage of sin. It cannot reign over us. We are called to obey now, not in order to enter into that liberty, but because God has already brought us into it! No one who is in Christ is still in Adam, defined by the reign of sin and death. It is simply a statement of fact.

The new creation—that is, the kingdom of God—has broken into "this present evil age" from the future ("the age to come"). Thus, the new life that Christians celebrate is not something that results from new resolutions, commitments, or schemes for a better life. It comes from God, not from us or from the possibilities that are already present in this age.

This two-age scheme (this present age / the age to come) governs Paul's thought. We find it already in Jesus' discourse in such places as Luke 18:30 ("in this time" / "in the age to come"); Luke 20:34–35 ("the sons of this age" versus the sons of "that age"); and Matthew 12:32 ("this age" / "the age to come"). This world of CNN, fashion, entertainment, consumerism, violence, and oppression—the world we take for granted as being the "real world"—is in truth the world that is passing away. It is the vain attempt of rebellious humanity to write its own script, to develop its own plot, and to find some meaning apart from God. Given that "this age" is easiest to treat as the real world because it is the one we encounter face-to-face every day, it will always be difficult to take "the age to come" as normative for us. But the resurrection of Christ, which is the harbinger of that future age here and now, tells us that our experience is simply wrong. That is great news!

We are already living in "these last days" (Hebrews 1:2; cf. Acts 2:17; James 5:3). And in this time between the two advents of our Lord, we experience the "already" and the "not yet." The "already" part of our salvation involves our being chosen in Christ, redeemed by him, forgiven, justified, regenerated, and sealed in him by his giving to us the promised Holy Spirit, who is the "down payment" on our final redemption (see Ephesians 1:3–14): "those whom he predestined he also called, and those whom he called he also justified, and those whom he justified he also glorified" (Romans 8:30). Even our glorification is such a certain reality that, although it lies in the future, it is included here in the list of accomplished facts. And so we pray, "Your will be done, on earth as it is in heaven" (Matthew 6:10). In heaven, our future is already present in Jesus Christ's being seated at his Father's right hand (see Hebrews 1:3), from where "he must reign until he has put all his enemies under his feet" (1 Corinthians 15:25; cf. Psalm 110:1; Acts 2:33–35), including the last enemy that is to be destroyed, which is death (see 1 Corinthians 15:26).

So there is no distinction between first-class (victorious) and second-class (carnal) Christians. There are only those who participate in "one Lord, one faith, one baptism" (Ephesians 4:5), and those who remain "dead in trespasses and sins" (Ephesians 2:1 NKJV). Thus, the believer is said to participate in "the powers of the age to come" through Word and Sacrament (Hebrews 6:5).

Of course, looks can be deceiving, especially when we see the signs of death, decay, sin, and evil all around us and, sadly, in our own lives. And yet, because we have been baptized into Christ (past tense), we can live in the Spirit (present tense) in hope of the glorification that awaits us (future tense). The Spirit unites us to Christ, taking that which belongs to him and making it ours day by day. There is a lot of "already" to the salvation God has accomplished for us. The new creation has dawned, and we have been incorporated into it.

Inward renewal (regeneration) will be followed by outward renewal (bodily resurrection):

> *So we do not lose heart. Though our outer nature is wasting away, our inner nature is being renewed day by day. For this slight momentary affliction is preparing for us an eternal weight of glory beyond all comparison, as we look not to the things that are seen but to the things that are unseen. For the things that are seen are transient, but the things that are unseen are eternal.*

2 Corinthians 4:16–18

This is why Scripture rather than our experience must determine our expectations. The inward renewal (new birth and sanctification) is usually much more difficult to detect with our senses than the "wasting away" of our bodies. The new creation is hidden under suffering, weakness, and decay, but we must take God's Word for it that the resurrection, this new creation, has two phases, and the first is well underway. We have been raised from death to life inwardly and will be raised bodily on the last day. Yet the current process of physical decay seems to witness against the new creation.

When my father was experiencing physical death at the most intense and rapid pace in his life, he was expressing his faith in ways I had never seen in him before. Ironically, while his body was least capable of evidencing this joy, paralyzed as it nearly was, he was most eager to show some bodily indication. Raising a finger heavenward, as if lifting a sack of cement, was something I never remember him doing before. In, with, and under his most debilitating physical condition, he was being inwardly renewed. In fact, it seemed that this inner renewal was keeping pace with the rapid experience of outward wasting. Aware of Paul's teaching here in 2 Corinthians 4:16, we were able as a family to interpret his experience as something more than mere tragedy.

I also saw this in Nicaragua, enjoying the hospitality of a pastor who had to fish for his meager wages. Together with his gracious wife and three children, he lived in a shack with a mud floor. Dinner was prepared on a grate on top of a tire, while a small pig scurried beneath our legs. I later learned the pastor had traveled a great distance to borrow a table and chairs for the occasion. Yet never have I enjoyed a more memorable meal and an even greater fellowship. Such experiences, read through the lens of God's story rather than that of this passing age, constantly confirm this teaching in 2 Corinthians 4:16

and elsewhere. God is doing something remarkable even in and through the temporary trials of this life. Regeneration is two-fold: the inner man and the outer man, the new birth through which we enter God's kingdom and the new creation that is God's kingdom in its consummated form.

"Not Yet" (Romans 7)

But then Romans 7 comes along to remind us of the "not yet" part of the equation. Whether we are talking about the individual believer or the kingdom of God more generally, there is a "not yet" that keeps us hoping for a fuller redemption. As marvelous as justification is, as precious as our new birth and sanctification are to us, as remarkable as the gains of Christ's kingdom may be in the world of sin and death—yet weakness, despair, frustration, struggle, and even failure are still too abundant for us to deny the reality of ongoing setbacks in the strife. Like Eastern religions, the mind-science groups in America (e.g., Christian Science, Scientology, and so forth) simply deny that evil, sin, and suffering really exist. Once we refuse to acknowledge their existence, we can no longer be their victims. But it is this belief, and not Christianity, that reflects a cowardly renunciation of reality. Scripture will not allow us to hide from the tragic dimension; instead, it calls us to take it with utmost seriousness.

There has been a great deal of debate in recent decades as to whether Paul is referring in Romans 7 to his own experience as a believer, as an unbeliever, or describing more generally the experience of Israel before and after the coming of Christ. But even if the "I" in Romans 7 is something *more* than Paul himself, it is surely not *less* than that, and Paul is surely not talking about his preconversion experience. After all, while he speaks in the present tense of his being "sold under sin" (7:14), he also says about himself what he elsewhere tells us cannot be said of any unregenerate person, namely, that in his sinning he nevertheless *wants to do the good.* "I have the desire to do what is right," he writes in verse 18. Indeed, he declares, "I delight in the law of God, in my inner being," even though "I see in my members another law waging war against the law of my mind" (7:22–23). Someone who is "dead in trespasses and sins" (Ephesians 2:1 NKJV) and who consequently "does not accept the things of the Spirit of God, for they are folly to him" (1 Corinthians 2:14) cannot be said to struggle in the way Paul declares he is struggling here: "I do not understand my own actions" (Romans 7:15). Because the things he said in Romans 6 are true, he expects victory over sin. And yet he finds that the war rages on. It is only because he is regenerate that he can have this real struggle against sin. And so the "already" of Romans 6 is somewhat qualified by this "not yet" of Romans 7.

Many challenges to the claim that Paul is here describing his own Christian experience have been motivated by theological difficulties with the apparent defeat that Paul sets before us. (After all, what search committee would call a pastor who conceded so much failure in his Christian life?) In the churches of my youth, Romans 7 was typically said to describe the "carnal Christian" as opposed to the believer who was "living in victory." Someone could be converted and begin to live the "victorious Christian life," but then fall into sin and suffer a setback. As a "backslider," such a person would still be saved but would be failing to live "the higher life."

But Paul is not presenting us with such a timeline here. The entire chapter is in the present tense. What the apostle seems to be saying, as shocking as it may be, is that every believer who is united to Christ is currently and *simultaneously* living in the "already" of chapter 6 and the "not yet" of chapter 7. Even as I seek to grow in godliness, pride crouches at the door, waiting to claim the prize. Even in my prayers, I can all too often identify with the hymn writer's words, "Prone to wander, Lord, I feel it, prone to leave the God I love." In moments of peak piety, I am still a struggling believer; and in moments of great transgression, I am still baptized into Christ's death and resurrection and thus a citizen of the new creation that has dawned with Christ's victory over sin and death and his sending of the Spirit. In this way, Romans 7 describes the *normal* Christian life! While it may intend more than this, it seems pretty clear that this is a crucial point of Paul's argument. Every believer is simultaneously in Romans 6, 7, and 8! Renowned Scottish preacher Alexander Whyte (1836–1921) is said to have repeatedly reminded his congregation, "As long as you are under my charge, you will never leave Romans 7."

While we never leave Romans 7 during this earthly pilgrimage, it is also worth being reminded that we also never leave Romans 6. Whatever progress someone is making in the Christian life and no matter how many setbacks he or she suffers, no matter how weak is someone's faith and repentance, each person who is united to Christ is already dead to sin and alive to righteousness. Paul here is reciting that cycle which Scripture and Christian experience teach only too well: the law accuses us and we die; the gospel raises us and we live; the law guides us in gospel-driven sanctification; and yet we find that our former master, sin, is trying desperately—even if finally unsuccessfully—to reclaim us, even by using God's law (unlawfully) to accomplish this. "It ain't over till it's over," and so we are always left hoping for more, for liberation not only from sin's guilt and tyranny but also from its very presence. The new creation—that kingdom of God in Christ—has come and has already swept us into its marvelous light. Yet it is present now in weakness and not yet in glory.

Look to Christ and Live in the Spirit (Romans 8:1–17)

But look at Christ! This is Paul's answer to his own disappointment with the quality of his Christian life. He answers his plaintive cry "who will deliver me from this body of death?" (7:24) with "thanks be to God through Jesus Christ our Lord!" (7:25). This marks the transition in his argument from the "not yet" of present victory over sin and death to the certainty of the hope that awaits us. Look to Christ! This is not a vague sentiment to "just trust God more" when things go wrong, but to pay attention to the historical fact that God has done something to and for and in this world in Jesus Christ that can never be undone and will only bear more fruit. He is "the firstfruits" of the full harvest (1 Corinthians 15:20–23). Paul is in effect saying, "See your head at the Father's right hand, your captain and brother directing the battle from his seat of victory." Paul's introspection in chapter 7 leads to despair; but when he looks outside himself to Christ, he is once again able to lift his head.

In this section (8:1–17), the apostle reasserts the "already" of chapter 6, the fact of the Spirit's inward activity here and now. Not only is Christ in heaven directing this warfare, but he has also sent his Spirit into our hearts to lead the ground campaign. And so this section begins by announcing again that "there is therefore now no condemnation for those who are in Christ Jesus" (8:1; cf. 5:1). Paul knows what fans a flickering candle into a dancing flame: a fresh glimpse of Christ and the gospel that indicates not only what God has done for our salvation, and what he is even now doing, but also what he will do in the future when he consummates his kingdom. What we need most in times of spiritual and physical trials are not more imperatives (our plans for our victory), but to be reminded again of the triumphant indicatives (God's plan for victory, achieved for us in Christ). Here, in Romans 8, Paul does not warn people about becoming "carnal Christians." He simply repeats the triumphant indicative: "You, however, *are not* in the flesh [that is, carnal] but in the Spirit, if in fact the Spirit of God dwells in you" (8:9, emphasis added).

"Flesh" and "Spirit" never mean for Paul an opposition between our bodies and souls. Rather, they represent human life under the dominion of sin and death (in the flesh) and human life under the dominion of righteousness and life (in the Spirit). Of course, in view here is the Holy Spirit and not our human spirits. The war between the flesh and the Spirit is cosmic in scope, but it is played out in our own individual lives as those who have been claimed by the Spirit in baptism and who yet await the consummation of the new creation. In the meantime, Paul says, take comfort in the fact that the Holy Spirit already indwells you and liberates you from "the spirit of slavery" that can cause you "to fall back into fear"; it is by the indwelling of God's Holy Spirit that we cry out "Abba! Father!" confirming that we have been adopted by God (8:15 – 17).

The Hope of Glory (Romans 8:18 – 30)

With all of this "already," we can await the "not yet" in full assurance. Here is how Paul lays this out before us:

> *For I consider that the sufferings of this present time are not worth comparing with the glory that is to be revealed to us. For the creation waits with eager longing for the revealing of the sons of God. For the creation was subjected to futility, not willingly, but because of him who subjected it, in hope that the creation itself will be set free from its bondage to decay and obtain the freedom of the glory of the children of God. For we know that the whole creation has been groaning together in the pains of childbirth until now. And not only the creation, but we ourselves, who have the firstfruits of the Spirit, groan inwardly as we wait eagerly for adoption as sons, the redemption of our bodies. For in this hope we were saved. Now hope that is seen is not hope. For who hopes for what*

he sees? But if we hope for what we do not see, we wait for it with patience.

Romans 8:18 – 25

This amazing passage links the salvation of individuals to the history of redemption. The great hope is not that our souls go to heaven when we die. The separation of soul and body at death is unnatural, part of the curse. Rather, we confess in the Nicene Creed, "I look for the resurrection of the body, and the life of the world to come." We cannot speak of "the real me" apart from our embodiment. This is why Paul links our final adoption to the resurrection of our bodies and not simply to the regeneration of the inner person.

The ancient Greeks ranked physical reality pretty low on the scale of being. The second-century Gnostics, attempting to recast Christianity in Greek categories of thought, went even further in opposing matter and spirit. Their goal was to escape "the late great planet Earth," to escape their bodies — "the prison house of the soul" — and the transitory history into which the supposedly innocent souls had been thrown.

How different is Paul's description here of the consummation that awaits us! Not only is our salvation incomplete until our bodies and souls are reunited in glorified and unified incorruptibility; it is incomplete until the whole creation shares the new creation with us! Adam was supposed to bring the human family into the everlasting Sabbath that God had promised with the Tree of Life. Instead, his rebellion drew the entire creation under the curse. By contrast, Christ, the second or last Adam, succeeded in this task and is now bringing with him not only "many sons" (males and females are included under this title) but also the whole creation.

Sometimes we are more Gnostic than Christian. We tend to think of salvation in terms of souls instead of whole persons ("soul winning," "saving souls," and so forth) and in terms of individual human beings to the exclusion of the cosmic scope of the redemption that actually awaits us. Salvation, according to Scripture, is not escape from our bodies or from the natural world, but the redemption of both. This is why the Christian life should not be seen in purely individualistic and "spiritual" (that is, nonmaterial) terms but as a foretaste of the glory that awaits us and all creation.

It is no wonder why the concept of heaven seems irrelevant, even to many Christians today. To the extent that it is seen as an escape from creation in all its "earthiness," the hope of heaven is really a denial of the goodness of what God has made and his plan for including it all in the new creation. Salvation is not the end of creation but its participation finally in the age to come, free of the bondage to which we human beings have subjected it.

Yet just as Paul tempered our enthusiasm over the announcement that we are forever free from the dominion of sin and death with the reality of his own ongoing struggle, now in chapter 8 he moves from the triumphant indicative of our future life to the reminder that "hope that is seen is not hope.... But if we hope for what we do not see, we wait for it with patience" (8:24–25). With both our individual sanctification and our stewardship of creation, we are neither defeatist (because of how much of the future consummation has already broken into our present) nor triumphalistic (because we wait patiently for Christ's return). Romans 6 challenges every form of defeatism, Romans 7 every form of triumphalism, and Romans 8 every form of escapism. We live in the tension of the "already" and "not yet" of our redemption. Christians strive against sin in the power of the Spirit, who has baptized us into Christ, and yet we know there will be weakness and frustration to the end, even as we also know that in the end we will wear the conqueror's crown.

This theology drives us outside of ourselves, first of all to God and secondly to our neighbors and the whole creation. We live for others. Gnostic piety is self-centered and purely introspective; biblical piety is chiefly extroverted. If the shape of final redemption is cosmic and not just individual, so too should be the shape of our hope as we relate to the world as citizens of "the age to come." It is not by monkish escape from the world and its problems but by humble service to Christ and our neighbor that we anticipate the second coming.

When asked what he would do if he knew that Jesus were to return the next day, Martin Luther is said to have replied, "I'd plant a tree." What he meant was that he would want Christ to find him fulfilling his calling in the world, for the good of his neighbors, out of the expectation that despite the look of things now, God will finally and forever liberate this world from its bondage. A doctor should wish to be found in the operating room, as God's means of holding back the inevitable curse of death, not as a denial of the resurrection but in view of it. A homemaker should be content to be found caring for her family in the countless routines of what can often seem mundane and insignificant. In this, she affirms life and anticipates the renewal of all things through faith, hope, and love.

Hope waits patiently, expectantly, confidently. While our feverish activity cannot bring about the promised consummation, either in relation to our own sanctification or to that of the creation more generally, we can — indeed, we must — keep our post wherever God has placed us in our callings as parents, children, employers, employees, friends, and neighbors. If it is only the salvation of souls that we are promised, planting a tree could be regarded as a distraction from a higher calling. Yet if it is this world that will join us in the triumphant procession into the full consummation of the age to come, our ordinary daily activity can become an arena for anticipating that day.

Even suffering can be a means of participating in the cross of Christ that will one day yield to our full fellowship in his glory: "For I consider that the sufferings of this present time are not worth comparing with the glory that is to be revealed to us" (Romans 8:18).

chapter nine
the true nature of spiritual warfare

In our brief marriage thus far, Lisa and I have been so overwhelmed with emergencies, it seems, that we have had trouble at times even relating to each other. From the first through the fourth years of our marriage — right up to my father's surgery — my wife suffered several difficult pregnancies, each leading to miscarriage. Each time, she was transformed by pregnancy-induced depression into a recluse, crying in bed with the shutters closed. Visits to my father's bedside only deepened her anxieties about God's nearness and goodness.

I wish I could say that these pressures drew us closer together; at times they actually threatened to pull us apart. I wish I could say I stood ready with answers when my wife needed them most; often I was oblivious to what she really should hear.

Finally, on September 16, 2002, James Paul was born. Almost immediately, the raging hormones subsided and the depression disappeared. It really was like night and day, and we were finally able to communicate again after months of wondering whether the next day would be as bleak as the last.

After a year of trying to conceive another child, the ultrasound revealed not one but three. Medical opinion told us we would be wise to abort. We refused. A difficult pregnancy ensued, bringing us to a serious dilemma in the twentieth week. We learned that one of the children was not growing at the same pace, and as the weeks wore on, it became clear that he was running out of nourishment. In the twenty-eighth week we were faced with the decision of whether to deliver all the babies three months prematurely, putting two developing lives at risk, or to allow the one child to die in order to give his healthy siblings the best chances of survival. After carefully weighing the medical case we'd been presented, praying, and seeking godly wisdom, we elected to have all three delivered the next morning.

Olivia, Matthew, and Adam were whisked away to the intensive care unit, where we were told that the first days were the most crucial, not only for Adam (at this point hanging on by a thread), but for the others as well. Bracing ourselves for the worst while praying and hoping for the best, we received a call in that first all-important week that Olivia had a "brain bleed." Yet subsequent scans showed no evidence of there ever having been one. Once again, God had shown us that we are entirely in his hands.

Although all of the children had troubles related to underdevelopment (especially breathing), it became clear as the weeks passed that Adam was the focus of our attention. Born at just over a pound, he experienced serious intestinal problems and was repeatedly brought back to health, only to suffer recurrences and new threats. Carefully untangling the web of tubes for food and blood, I would place Adam on my chest and wonder how such a fragile life could survive the night. It reminded me of the hamster I had growing up that I would rest on my chest. Although he was my son, this child was barely larger than that childhood pet (that is, when Adam's legs were fully extended). After visiting the intensive care unit for three months (two months for Olivia and Matthew), we were finally able to rejoice in the homecoming of Adam.

And now, after healed fractures and successful surgeries (and a freak accident that landed him back in the ICU just after his second birthday), Adam has a clean bill of health along with the others. We still do not have any idea why God allowed us to go through all of this right on the heels of my father's death and mother's stroke. At the time, it seemed that Satan was having some success in pulling us under just as we were keeping our nose above the waves of doubt and depression.

Kingdoms in Conflict

As this book has already noted, there is a cosmic battle between the kingdoms of God and Satan, and our lives are part of that unfolding drama. While we dare not reduce our physical suffering to spiritual battle, we must also not miss this important aspect of all suffering. The story I've just recounted illustrates this. During such ordeals, we are put on trial, like Job and our Lord, with Satan taking up the role of prosecutor and Christ as our defense attorney. Satan's objective in this contest is to undermine our confidence in God's merciful will toward us, while God's is to strengthen it.

Just as physical battles involve spiritual ones, it works in the reverse as well. A friend called me a number of years ago about a young man who was going through some sort of personal crisis, wondering if I might meet with him, especially since he was eager to talk about what he was picking up from my book *Putting Amazing Back into Grace.* Over lunch when I was in his area, he told me that, in spite of a strong Christian upbringing and faith in Christ, he wondered if he was gay. It became clear to me in our conversation that he was *not* gay, but a Christian struggling with homosexual temptation. First of all, he *worried* that he might be gay. This is a rudimentary sign of repentance, unlike those who consider themselves gay — that is, who affirm their homosexual lifestyle. Further, he professed faith in Christ not only for freedom from sin's guilt but also from its tyranny. He wanted to be liberated from this sinful tendency.

The problem was that his pastor did not see it this way, telling this young man that he had been "given over," as Paul described the condition of the unregenerate heart (Romans 1:28). This pastor had interpreted "given over" as a reference to homosexual desire, while Paul actually treated homosexuality there (1:24–27) as an example of what becomes socially acceptable when the knowledge of God is eclipsed. In other words, according to Romans, "given over" does not describe those who struggle with homosexuality; rather, homosexuality is an example of what is acceptable when we reject God. By the way, Paul also mentions covetousness, gossip, disrespect, and heartlessness, among other things (1:29–31).

This young man clearly did not reject God, but his pastor had rejected him, although he was not officially excommunicated. Sadly, his parents, leading supporters of conservative "family values" causes, were embarrassed by their son and accepted their pastor's verdict.

Through subsequent correspondence and phone conversations, the young man and I were able to talk through some of these issues. Most often, what this young brother needed was absolution — the constant affirmation and assurance that he was forgiven of his sins for the sake of Christ. Only forgiveness can lead to what is called *evangelical* (that is, gospel) repentance rather than merely *legal* (that is, fear-inspired) repentance. He eventually moved out to our organization's offices in California as a volunteer to help others find this amazing grace.

Returning home after a year with us, he found himself trapped again in a cycle of condemnation-guilt-transgression. He finally decided to end it all by taking his own life. I have no doubt where he is right now. But he remains for me a symbol of the tragedy of bad theology, and the tragedies it produces in the most practical ways. We need to recognize again and again that it is only the gospel—the sight of Christ in his saving office—that can give us faith and also genuine obedience. Commands and threats are part of Scripture; we need to acknowledge them, and if we do so, we will more deeply feel our need for Christ. But commands and threats—even if nicely issued as helpful suggestions—cannot fill our sails with faith, hope, and love. Apart from the gospel, the law is the most terrible burden and leads us to either despair or the delusion of self-righteousness.

Nearly everyone knows Saint Augustine, that fourth-century giant, as the doctor of grace. To a large extent, the Reformation was simply a recovery of and improvement on Augustine's system. Few quills have graced the subject of guilt and grace like the Bishop of Hippo's. And yet, Augustine's own conversion was not so much due to the guilt of his sins as to their power. Resting in his garden, the immoral young pagan heard a child singing, "Take up and read, take up and read." So, locating a New Testament, he turned randomly to Romans 13:13–14 (NIV): "Let us behave decently, as in the daytime, not in orgies and drunkenness, not in sexual immorality and debauchery, not in dissension and jealousy. Rather, clothe yourselves with the Lord Jesus Christ, and do not think about how to gratify the desires of the sinful nature." A member of a heretical sect known for its immorality, the young and lustful Augustine was under the tyranny of sin. The gospel promised to free him from bondage to himself. Clothed with Christ, Augustine found a way out.

What do all these stories share in common? They point up, in quite different ways, the interconnectedness of body and soul, and therefore of physical and spiritual battle. Job's own personal holocaust drove him to doubt God's goodness and concern for him; at times he even seemed to come close to surrendering the conviction that in the end justice would be done. Life's crises, whether they start out as physical or spiritual, end up involving the whole person in any case.

A Status Report on the Cosmic Battle

Spiritual warfare has become a hot topic in Christian circles in recent decades, generating scores of books, conferences, and tapes on such themes as breaking generational curses, identifying by name the specific demons controlling various maladies (the demon of poverty, of alcoholism, of lust, and so forth), and forming prayer rallies for binding evil spirits. A new vocabulary has emerged around this spiritual technology, centering on the "spiritual mapping" of "territorial spirits." But is this biblical spirituality, science fiction, or superstition?

Many of these writings verge on what is called cosmological dualism — that is, the belief that the universe is in the grip of a cosmic duel between God and Satan, as if these represented two equal forces. Of course, Scripture does teach that there is a cosmic duel, as I have been arguing throughout this book. But are we in a tug-of-war in which we as believers decide the outcome? Or is it the case that, as Luther was fond of saying, even the devil is God's devil?

In Scripture, the recurring polemic against the idolatry of the nations is that they believe in many gods and lords, each ruling a particular area of life, while Israel's God alone is Lord of all. There cannot be two sovereigns in the universe. But Satan has always been a pretender. Since his infamous treason, he has always fancied himself a deity in his own right. And to the extent that human beings are seduced by his deceit, they are under his immediate dominion, even though God alone is ultimately King.

It is true that Satan is described as "the god of this world" (2 Corinthians 4:4). Yet far from serving as a proof text for our collective exorcism of territorial demons and generational curses, Paul goes on to give us the sense in which he intends the phrase. First of all, "god of this world" has to do not with spiritual technology but with the gospel:

> And even if our gospel is veiled, it is veiled only to those who are perishing. In their case the god of this world has blinded the minds of the unbelievers, to keep them from seeing the light of the gospel of the glory of Christ, who is the image of God. For what we proclaim is not ourselves, but Jesus Christ as Lord.

2 Corinthians 4:3–4

In other words, Satan has deluded the world into denying the God who has made them, and then when the Redeemer is proclaimed, the world rejects him now as it did when he appeared (see John 14–16). In other words, we are dealing here in the realm of faith and unbelief, not magic.

If we could simply coordinate prayer armies to bring down the territorial spirits, the campaign against Satan and his hosts would be easy. But it is much more difficult, because the problem is not external to us, but internal. The problem is not that we are held in bondage against our will, longing for someone to name and claim our victory, but that we are willing captives and refuse to trust in God apart from his intervening grace.

Jesus made this point when the religious leaders of Israel thought that evil was something outside of them, specifically, the occupying forces of the Romans. He told them they were children of sin, even though they prided themselves on being Abraham's children:

> They said to him, "We were not born of sexual immorality. We have one Father—even God."

> *Jesus said to them, "If God were your Father, you would love me, for I came from God and I am here.... It is because you cannot bear to hear my word. You are of your father the devil, and your will is to do your father's desires."*
>
> John 8:41–44

Notice again the reference to God's word. This is the battleground of spiritual warfare. Preferring Satan's enticements to glory instead of God's word, Adam plunged the race into sin. And the second Adam, in his own trial, was tempted with the glory of the world. Satan focused on Jesus' immediate needs. But instead Jesus answered, "Man shall not live by bread alone, but by every word that comes from the mouth of God" (Matthew 4:4). Just as Paul linked Satan's dominion to the world's blindness to God's word, so Jesus did in these passages.

The most exciting and liberating thing a believer can hear in the middle of spiritual and physical distress is not that there is a secret battle plan for defeating the powers of darkness if we will only come together and follow its failproof steps, but the announcement that Jesus Christ has already accomplished this for us in his first advent. After Jesus sent out the seventy-two disciples into the harvest, they returned elated: "Lord, even the demons are subject to us in your name!" Jesus replied, "I saw Satan fall like lightning from heaven," giving them authority over Satan and his minions who blind the world. "Nevertheless," Jesus added, "do not rejoice in this, that the spirits are subject to you, but rejoice that your names are written in heaven" (Luke 10:17–20).

A clear theme is emerging here: the binding of Satan and the powers of darkness occurs with the arrival of the kingdom. It centers on the spiritual blindness of which the physical restoration of sight is but a sign. The healings and exorcisms performed by Jesus and his apostles are signposts announcing that the kingdom of the gospel has finally arrived: "But if it is by the Spirit of God that I cast out demons," Jesus declares, "then the kingdom of God has come upon you. Or how can someone enter a strong man's house and plunder his goods, unless he first binds the strong man?" (Matthew 12:28–29). It is not an appeal to a general program for our defeat of Satan but the confession of Jesus as "the Christ, the Son of the living God" (Matthew 16:16) that evokes Jesus' further announcement (verses 18–19): "And I tell you, you are Peter, and on this rock I will build my church, and the gates of hell shall not prevail against it. I will give you the keys of the kingdom of heaven, and whatever you bind on earth shall be bound in heaven, and whatever you loose on earth shall be loosed in heaven."

The authority to bind and loose is exercised wherever and whenever the gospel is proclaimed, wherever the devil's fortress is looted and his prisoners are baptized, transferred from the kingdom of sin and death to the kingdom of life everlasting. The cosmic battle, according to the Gospels, turns on faith in Christ and admission to his kingdom. Spiritual warfare is all about the gospel. It is when Peter's confession is heard on the lips of men, women, and children from Jerusalem to the ends of the earth that we see the sun setting on Satan's empire.

In short, then, this is the status report from the battlefield: Satan is bound, under house arrest. And yet, like a Mafia boss in prison, he still manages to cause trouble. As Revelation 12 captures in a marvelously condensed snapshot of this war, Satan has been cast out of heaven but vigorously pursues retaliation against the church that has been liberated from his fortress.

Shields and Swords

But let us focus on the principal proof text often adduced for the various approaches to spiritual warfare that seem to have more in common with science fiction than with Scripture. Our goal is not simply to refute error but to explore the rich meaning of spiritual warfare from this passage in an effort to understand its true nature. The text I have in mind is from Ephesians 6:

> *Finally, be strong in the Lord and in the strength of his might. Put on the whole armor of God, that you may be able to stand against the schemes of the devil. For we do not wrestle against flesh and blood, but against the rulers, against the authorities, against the cosmic powers over this present darkness, against the spiritual forces of evil in the heavenly places. Therefore take up the whole armor of God, that you may be able to withstand in the evil day, and having done all, to stand firm. Stand therefore, having fastened on the belt of truth, and having put on the breastplate of righteousness, and, as shoes for your feet, having put on the readiness given by the gospel of peace. In all circumstances take up the shield of faith, with which you can extinguish all the flaming darts of the evil one; and take the helmet of salvation, and the sword of the Spirit, which is the word of God, praying at all times in the Spirit, with all prayer and supplication. To that end keep alert with all perseverance, making supplication for all the saints, and also for me, that words may be given to me in opening my mouth boldly to proclaim the mystery of the gospel, for which I am an ambassador in chains, that I may declare it boldly, as I ought to speak.*

Ephesians 6:10–20

The Old Testament background of this apostolic exhortation is probably Isaiah 59, and Ephesians 6 is filled with allusions to it. A brief survey of that prophetic passage will therefore open up Paul's teaching on spiritual warfare in Ephesians.

First of all, the language of Isaiah 59 evokes a courtroom scene, a usual context for the prophets, since they were attorneys of the covenant. Unlike our own system, there was no division of labor between the prosecution and the defense. The prophets as covenant lawyers represented both parties in the suit—both the offended party (God) and the transgressors (the people of Israel). The people are summoned to court.

Second, taking the preceding chapters and contemporary prophets (especially Jeremiah and Hosea) into account, we know that the people had justified themselves throughout the ordeal. They had seen the destruction of Jerusalem and their exile not as the wages of sin but as a breach of promise on God's part. Thus, they had put God on trial, to be judged by their experience.

Instead, God holds up his word as the standard and turns the tables. The two perennial charges humanity lodges against God in times of suffering are that he is either unable or unwilling to save them. In other words, either his sovereignty or his goodness has to go. But Yahweh's case is presented by his attorney: "Behold, the LORD's hand is not shortened, that it cannot save, or his ear dull, that it cannot hear; but your iniquities have made a separation between you and your God, and your sins have hidden his face from you so that he does not hear" (Isaiah 59:1–2). People have claimed that either God's arm is too short to reach into this world and save his people, or he has bad hearing. Whether it is his arm or his ears, God is not of much comfort to his people in their distress. He is the problem, not the solution.

But the prophet reverses the charges.

Third, the case against the people is prosecuted by damning testimony, not merely from victims of their oppression and injustice, but from their own persons. Like a criminal who doesn't even know how to cover his tracks, Israel's "hands are defiled with blood and your fingers with iniquity; your lips have spoken lies; your tongue mutters wickedness" (59:3). Exhibit A is Israel's own collective body. It is not God's arm or ears that are at fault, but Israel's hands, fingers, lips, and tongue that declare their guilt.

The prophet continues by referring to unjust lawsuits and corrupt courts, lying and deceit. It was "every person for himself," we might say. They are likened to venomous snakes or spiders that weave their web of corruption and then use it to cover themselves, hiding their treachery under a cloak of self-righteousness: "Their webs will not serve as clothing; [they] will not cover themselves with what they make. Their works are works of iniquity, and deeds of violence are in their hands" (59:6). They do not simply fall into the wrong crowd and make honest mistakes. Instead, their own persons are used as evidence against them: "Their feet run to evil, and they are swift to shed innocent blood; their thoughts are thoughts of iniquity; desolation and destruction are in their highways." They crave war rather than peace (59:7–8).

When we think about our own nation, one need not be a political partisan to experience a wounded conscience. Although we hold ourselves up to the world as its only hope for freedom, justice, and opportunity, we lead the world statistically in debt, violence, and crime. One in every twenty-seven men in America today is incarcerated, and that tragic statistic is far higher for African-Americans. When the prophets talk about the powers and principalities of this present evil age, they are not thinking in science-fiction terms. They have in mind the concrete, systematic, and institutionalized forms of bondage that sin forms over time.

But ultimately this is a spiritual problem rooted first of all in sin — humanity's collective refusal to answer to God, which reflects its willing bondage to the powers of darkness in the heavenly places. We see this fact in the next remarkable speech of the prophet, who now addresses the court in the name of the people rather than the King: "Therefore justice is far from us, and righteousness does not overtake us" (59:9a). *We* are the problem. God has not been unfaithful to his promises; we have: "We hope for light, and behold, darkness, and for brightness, but we walk in gloom. We grope for the wall like the blind; we grope like those who have no eyes; we stumble at noon as in the twilight, among those in full vigor we are like [the] dead" (59:9b–10). It is not simply that the people have failed to *do* what is right; they have so successfully suppressed the truth in unrighteousness that they no longer *know* right from wrong.

This is not posed as a problem for only some of the people. It's not just "those people over there" or "that political party" but each individual who has lost all sense of God's holiness, glory, justice, righteousness, and awe. Justice and salvation are "far from us," Isaiah says, because "our transgressions are multiplied before you, and our sins testify against us; for our transgressions are with us, and we know our iniquities" (59:11b–12). It begins with an ignorance of and indifference to God (59:13a)—something that is all too common even in our churches today, where the focus is on us and our happiness. It extrapolates into a cancer that threatens the life of the whole body, to the point where "justice is turned back, and righteousness stands afar off; for truth has stumbled in the public squares, and uprightness cannot enter. Truth is lacking, and he who departs from evil makes himself a prey" (59:14–15).

We would not be wrong to hear echoes in this passage of the fall itself in Eden. This is where Satan sets up his battlements and builds his ramparts: God and his word are not to be trusted; instead, be your own boss, find your own path, believe in yourself, and be true to yourself. Israel's trial in the wilderness and in the Promised Land is a recapitulation of Adam's trial in the garden, just as Jesus' was of both, undoing by his own obedience

the sin of Adam and Israel and bringing down on his own head
the curses of our covenant breaking.

And this is precisely where Isaiah 59 itself turns from judgment to justification, from bad news to good news:

> *The LORD saw it, and it displeased him*
> *   that there was no justice.*
> *He saw that there was no [one],*
> *   and wondered that there was no one to intercede;*
> *then his own arm brought him salvation,*
> *   and his righteousness upheld him.*
> *He put on righteousness as a breastplate,*
> *   and a helmet of salvation on his head;*
> *he put on garments of vengeance for clothing,*
> *   and wrapped himself in zeal as a cloak.*
> *According to their deeds, so will he repay,*
> *   wrath to his adversaries, repayment to his enemies;*
> *   to the coastlands he will render repayment.*
> *So they shall fear the name of the LORD from the west,*
> *   and his glory from the rising of the sun;*
> *for he will come like a rushing stream,*
> *   which the wind of the LORD drives.*
> *"And a Redeemer will come to Zion,*
> *   to those in Jacob who turn from transgression,"*
> *declares the LORD.*

Isaiah 59:15b–20

The good news is twofold: (1) justice will be done; liberation will come; righteousness will be vindicated; evil, oppression, and violence will be wiped off the face of the earth; and (2) all who repent and turn to the Redeemer will be saved.

This courtroom trial in Isaiah 59 does not say there is a one-to-one correspondence between suffering and specific sins we have committed. We have already seen in Job that this is an inadequate theology. Sin is much more complicated than that, being likened here to a spider's web that is woven not just by each of us but by all of us collectively. Thus, we are all simultaneously sinners and sinned-against, perpetrators and victims. We are caught in the very web we help make, and instead of undoing this cycle of violence, unrighteousness, injustice, and suffering, we willingly participate in it. This is the truth about all of us. That is why the only good news in this trial is that the Judge himself—whom the transgressors had originally arraigned—takes off his robe and dons the warrior's suit. It is Yahweh the King himself whose righteousness upholds him—and us—bringing justice and justification in his train.

Our Captain's Armor

In Ephesians 6, then, Paul draws on this cosmic trial and relates it to our own individual Christian experience. Satan comes to us, as he came to Adam, Israel, and Jesus, promising the kingdoms of this world if we will serve him. Those who have renounced Satan and his lies are targeted for persecution, temptation, and suffering. All we have—and it is enough—are the weapons God has provided.

Notice that the military dress and weapons Paul lists are identical to those mentioned by Isaiah—with one crucial difference. In Isaiah 59, they are worn by Yahweh himself, the Redeemer who comes to Zion. In Ephesians 6, they are worn by us. This is what Paul means earlier in the letter, when he tells us to "put off [our] old self" and to "put on the new self" (Ephesians 4:22, 24), and elsewhere to "put on the Lord Jesus Christ" (Romans 13:14; Galatians 3:27; see also Romans 6:6; Colossians 3:9–15).

None of these defenses mentioned are our own. We do not read here about our marvelous Christian experience, our love for the saints, our progress in obedience, our passion for God.

We certainly do not read here (or elsewhere, for that matter) of elaborate schemes for identifying and binding territorial spirits or generational curses. To be sure, we find calls to obedience in Scripture, and heeding these is an unmistakable mark of a Christian. But they are not the Christian's *defenses* in wartime. Every item mentioned in Paul's list is external to us. Donning someone else's armor, we are standing in someone else's strength. The testimony that prevails in this battle is not about us and what we have done or how we have improved, but a witness to God and what he has done in Christ. Pointing away from ourselves to Christ is the only sure defense when Satan accuses us in God's courtroom.

There is the belt of truth (Ephesians 6:14). How can we answer the devil's accusations and twisting of Scripture if we do not ourselves know God's truth? As we have seen in the story above about the young man who took his life, knowing the truth is a life-or-death affair. Bad theology can literally kill someone, physically, even as it takes the spiritual lives of so many. Sound doctrine is not, as many seem to assume today, a distraction from the real life of Christian discipleship, but preparation for it.

Then there is the breastplate of righteousness that we wear (6:14) — that "alien righteousness," as Luther called it, Christ's own righteousness imputed to us, although we are wicked in ourselves. This righteousness alone stands in God's judgment and therefore in the face of Satan's accusations. After all, Satan is often right when he accuses us, and he terrifies our conscience with the fear that we have fallen out of favor with God. If somehow he can undermine our faith in Christ and the sufficiency of his righteousness, what could constitute a more sterling victory? But he cannot succeed in this if we are wearing Christ's righteousness and not relying on our naked chest to preserve us from his blows.

Next, the gospel of peace is our shoes that make us ready to run the race set before us (6:15). Like the belt of truth and breastplate of righteousness, the gospel is not about us but about someone else: Christ and his proclamation, "It is finished!"

Further, Satan cannot penetrate the shield of faith (6:16). If we were to do battle with our experience, our intellect, or our works, we would fall quickly, but faith, too, points away from ourselves to Christ, who intercedes for us.

Finally, Paul mentions the sword of the Spirit, which is not a fanciful light-saber to be wielded by spiritual heroes but is nothing else than "the word of God" (6:17). Nothing in us or done by us is victorious in spiritual battle. We can only extinguish the flaming arrows of doubt, fear, and anxiety by directing the world, the flesh, and the devil to our Captain at the Father's right hand, who has crushed the devil's head and rendered his accusations and efforts futile.

With all of this in mind, Paul concludes by encouraging his readers to continually pray "for all the saints," not just for themselves (6:18). He asks prayers for himself, not just because of his apostolic importance, nor indeed that he would be kept from all suffering, but in order "that words may be given to me in opening my mouth boldly to proclaim the mystery of the gospel, for which I am an ambassador in chains, that I may declare it boldly, as I ought to speak" (6:19–20). This does not mean that we should not pray for a whole host of other things, *including* tangible physical needs. But it does mean that even the role of prayer in spiritual warfare centered for Paul on the progress of this gospel of Christ to the ends of the earth. This, after all, is how Satan's kingdom is crushed and the kingdom of grace comes to reign in its ashes.

The Main Event

When trouble comes, whether external or internal threats to our physical or spiritual welfare, we are to turn inside out.

Our first inclination at these times is the opposite. Like a turtle withdrawing into its shell at the sign of danger, we turn inward and grab hold of our own resources to sustain us. But as counterintuitive as it is for us, we must turn outward at precisely these times and hope only in the Lord, whatever our conscience threatens, whatever blandishments Satan offers, whatever our experience tells us is the obvious case.

One thing that made sense to my wife during her trials, she now says, was my encouragement to concentrate not on what she was going through but on what God is doing in this cosmic battle of the ages. Especially when our infants were in intensive care for three months, the obvious temptation was to be so completely preoccupied with them that we lost sight of God and his grace in Jesus Christ. This has helped us now to put our children in a more proper perspective: we must fulfill our responsibilities as parents to the best of our ability, but at the end of the day they belong to the Lord, and they are in his hands. What *we* are going through is not the main event; it is rather what God is up to as he incorporates us into this war of the ages.

The seventeenth-century theologian John Owen once made this observation:

> When Christ comes with his spiritual power on the soul, to conquer it to himself, he hath no quiet landing place. He can set foot on no ground, but what he must fight for and conquer. Not the mind, not an affection, not the will, but all is secured against him. And when grace hath made its entrance, yet sin will dwell in all its coastlands.[1]

We will not grow without a fight, without sharing in Christ's sufferings. Unlike justification, our sanctification is a lifelong struggle—so much for "let go and let God." Small victories are prized; battles lost are soon forgotten, extracting lessons for the next. None of our enemies—the world, the flesh, or the devil—will simply move aside and put up a white flag. And yet, in our fighting we fail to hide our unrestrained anticipation prefigured in the arrival of Israel in the Promised Land, when at last the land will be at rest from war. Until then, we fight as those who belong to the Warrior-God, who has already conquered with his own right arm.

Paul's best word on the subject may actually be found in Romans 8:

> *What then shall we say to these things? If God is for us, who can be against us? He who did not spare his own Son but gave him up for us all, how will he not also with him graciously give us all things? Who shall bring any charge against God's elect? It is God who justifies. Who is to condemn? Christ Jesus is the one who died—more than that, who was raised—who is at the right hand of God, who indeed is interceding for us. Who shall separate us from the love of Christ? Shall tribulation, or distress, or persecution, or famine, or nakedness, or danger, or sword? As it is written,*

> *"For your sake we are being killed all the day long;*
> *we are regarded as sheep to be slaughtered."*

> *No, in all these things we are more than conquerors through him who loved us. For I am sure that neither death nor life, nor angels nor rulers, nor things present nor things to come, nor powers, nor height nor depth, nor anything else in all creation, will be able to separate us from the love of God in Christ Jesus our Lord.*

> Romans 8:31–39

Let this be your confidence on the bed of affliction or the fearful waves of doubt, and you will stand firm in the day of battle. Christ is enough, even for you.

chapter ten
when GOD goes to a funeral

It was my turn to preach in chapel. At the beginning of the semester each of us on the faculty had been assigned to speak on one of the miracles of Christ. The passage I had been given was John 11:1–44.

In God's providence, my time slot came just two days after my dad finally breathed his last. In conjunction with chapel that day, we held a memorial service. As I spoke about Jesus raising Lazarus from the grave, I felt it would touch our seminary community, as well as family and friends, gathered for different reasons but each with his or her own challenges in life.

The raising of Lazarus is a climactic sign in John's gospel. Contrary to what we often see on TV's religious broadcasting, the purpose of Jesus' great works was not to dazzle, or even to prove Christ's divinity in some abstract manner, as one might prove one's psychic powers by bending a spoon without touching it. Jesus' miracles are *signs*, not just *wonders*. Signs point to something else. They are not the point, but the pointer. Jesus heals on the Sabbath and then proclaims himself "Lord of the Sabbath." He feeds the five thousand and then announces that he is "the Bread of Life" whose flesh is real food unto eternal life.

The problem is that the onlookers typically go no further than the sign. They do not care about the thing signified. Lost in the illustration, they forget the point that the illustration was intended to help convey. At the feeding of the five thousand, the crowds are amazed by the provision of their felt needs, but when Jesus begins to teach them who he is, it becomes clear that they are interested in the gifts more than the giver. Here the most climactic and demonstrative sign, the raising of Lazarus, also leads to the most demonstrative reaction against him by the religious leaders.

Death of a Loved One (John 11:1 – 16)

Lazarus, along with his sisters, was a close friend of Jesus. They made their home a base for Jesus' Jerusalem-area mission, since Bethany was something like a suburb, only an hour's walk away. "It was [*that*] Mary who anointed the Lord," and Jesus was entreated to come to his ill friend's side when Mary identified him to Jesus as "he whom you love" (11:2 – 3). The assumption here is that Jesus and Lazarus were so close that all Jesus needed was to be told of his condition. Surely Jesus would come running.

The sisters' plea for Jesus was not wrong, but shortsighted in its motivation. They were appealing to him for the healing of Lazarus, while Jesus anticipated using his friend's death as an opportunity to signify his person and work. It was not about Lazarus, but about Jesus: "I am the resurrection and the life" (11:25). Again we think of the difference between the theology of glory and the theology of the cross. It is not wrong to anticipate glory — both God's and our own participation in it — but the problem comes when we think that our own immediate concerns are ultimate: God, if he is our friend, must provide for us or our loved ones in such and such a manner.

Mary and Martha knew that Jesus *could* heal their failing brother and simply assumed that, given his love for Lazarus, Jesus would *want* to. Here we return to that conundrum: Is God both sovereign (able to heal) and good (willing to heal)? If the healing doesn't occur, one of these affirmations comes into question, we reason. If Jesus really loves Lazarus, he'll come quickly. "God, if you really care about me, _____"—fill in your own blank.

In the thick of trouble, this is not so bad a response. In fact, it is a sign of faith on the sisters' part: God can and will heal. Rather, the problem is in the timing and the terms. "It is for the glory of God," says Jesus, "so that the Son of God may be glorified through it" (11:4). In terms of the unfolding plot, Lazarus is a character in Jesus' story, not vice versa. The glorification of the Son as the Messiah is the real "show" here, as was the case with all of the miracles. They are signs, not ends in themselves.

Jesus deliberately delays his return to Bethany two more days. What could have been happening in the sisters' minds during these two agonizing days? They had no idea what Jesus was going to do—something far greater than they had asked him to do. With the wisdom and data at their disposal, they could only have been utterly depressed at the apparent lack of response on Jesus' part. He had acted promptly before: in healing Jairus's daughter (Luke 8) and in raising the widow's son in the middle of the funeral procession (Luke 7). How callous could he be if he healed perfect strangers but would not rush to the aid of one of his closest friends?

With the plot centered around Jesus, however, John's gospel points up some important pieces of data we may otherwise miss. First of all, verses 7–16 make it clear that a return to Judea meant renewed conflict with the religious leaders. "The disciples said to him, 'Rabbi, the Jews were just now seeking to stone you, and are you going there again?'"(11:8). He tells them, "Our friend Lazarus has fallen asleep, but I go to awaken him," to which the disciples (no doubt concerned about their own safety) reply, "Lord, if he has fallen asleep, he will recover" (11:11, 12). "Then Jesus told them plainly, 'Lazarus has died, and for your sake I am glad that I was not there, so that you may believe. But let us go to him'" (11:14–15).

Nobody—the disciples, Lazarus, Mary, or Martha—nobody but Jesus knew why he had allowed Lazarus to die in the first place, especially if all along he was going to visit him eventually. It was all palpably confusing to their experience. It simply did not make sense. Then there is that odd comment from Thomas: "Let us also go, that we may die with him" (11:16). Whether he was being sarcastic or serious, the assumption is that returning to Bethany in Judea meant death, not life. It would be the end of the road.

Jesus' cryptic remark, "For your sake I am glad that I was not there, so that you may believe," could not be discerned this side of the events in Bethany. It could only be clear to them after the completion of the episode, not within it. This is a crucial point for our own application in such circumstances. From their perspective, in terms of their own experience, the sisters (and Lazarus in his final hours) and the disciples would have logically concluded that Jesus, whom they had seen as perfectly capable of healing, was simply callous. He was uninterested, unconcerned. Their experience was not irrational or illogical, but rather incomplete and therefore inadequate to sit in judgment on God's ways. Just as the sisters were too shortsighted to really see what Jesus was doing with Lazarus, the disciples (especially Thomas) were too shortsighted to really see what Jesus was doing by going to Jerusalem: dying and rising. In the disciples' perspective, he should be going to Jerusalem for "victory," triumph, conquest, just as he should have come to Bethany.

Lazarus *had* to die in order for the greater miracle to occur. There is something more important than the healing of his friend. Jesus knew the great work he would accomplish in the power of the Spirit when he came finally to Bethany. It is like Elijah pouring water on the fire pit, just to make sure God's glorious power will be obvious. As the greater Elijah, Jesus was engaged in a cosmic contest between Yahweh and the serpent. That was the larger story behind all these other stories.

Confrontation with His Loved Ones (11:17 – 27)

After a four-day interval between Lazarus's death and Jesus' arrival in Bethany, Martha displays the sort of frustration one would not have expected a woman of her day to show toward a man in public, much less a rabbi. Yet, after scolding Jesus for his tardiness — "Lord, if you had been here, my brother would not have died" — she immediately adds, "But even now I know that whatever you ask from God, God will give you" (11:21 – 22). Martha's faith in Jesus is unfailing. He can still turn things around — even after her brother's entombment: "even now …"

It is important to see how Martha here reflects that combination of heart-wrenching disappointment and faith that we find in the Psalms. She does not believe that even death has the last say in the presence of Jesus, which is thus far more faith than we have seen in the Twelve. Martha's theology is right. Evidently, she believes in the resurrection of the dead, as many Jews (at least the Pharisees) did. But it's like Philip saying to Jesus, "Lord, show us the Father," with Jesus' reply, "Whoever has seen me has seen the Father" (John 14:8, 9). In fact, the scene there is similar. There, Jesus announces that he is the Way, the Truth, and the Life (14:6) — not simply someone who can lead to truth and life, but the Truth and Life in person. Philip asks for something more, but Jesus replies, "Whoever has seen me has seen the Father."

Jesus *is* the Resurrection and the Life. He is the source of life beyond the grave. Jesus responds to Martha, "Your brother will rise again" (11:23). "Do you believe this?" (11:26). Jesus presses her to commit herself, not just to the theological *question* of resurrection of the dead, but to *him as the Resurrection and the Life*! To claim to be "the Resurrection and the Life" or "the Way, and the Truth, and the Life" is to claim nothing less than equality with the Father. So now the stakes of Martha's confession are raised considerably. In the presence of witnesses, she is called not only to declare that Jesus can raise the dead, as Elijah had done; Jesus calls on her to acknowledge that he is himself the God on whom Elijah called. He not only can *give* life; he *is* Life. This is a very large step.

One of the marvelous clauses here is "though he die" (11:25). It is one thing to halt the processes of decay and death; it is quite another to bring someone back to life. Jesus declares of himself, "I am the resurrection and the life. Whoever believes in me, though he die, yet shall he live, and everyone who lives and believes in me shall never die. Do you believe this?" (11:25 – 26).

Now Jesus is not simply asking Martha to confess that Lazarus will live, but that those who trust in Jesus Christ — even though they die — will be raised to never die again. It's no longer about Lazarus per se. Jesus is calling Martha into the circle of that cosmic trial between Yahweh and the serpent, calling her to be a witness (the Greek word for *witness* is the same as for *martyr*). Lazarus's resurrection will be a sign — proof, in fact — of that reality to be inaugurated with Christ's own resurrection from the dead. Even though people will still die despite the arrival of Messiah, they will not remain dead forever but will be raised in the likeness not of Lazarus's mortal body (still tending toward death) but of Christ's glorified body.

Martha's answer on the witness stand, racked with myriad thoughts and feelings of desperation and hope, brought Job's up-to-date: "She said to him, 'Yes, Lord; I believe that you are the Christ, the Son of God, who is coming into the world'" (11:27). This is the big event in Bethany this day. Without discounting the resurrection of Lazarus still to come in the story, we cannot forget that, as with all of Jesus' miracles, the most amazing thing is the reality that the sign merely announces and the confession it draws from our lips. In the midst of his agony, Job cries out, "I know that my Redeemer lives, and ... in my flesh I shall see God" (Job 19:25–26). This is the faith that perseveres through the contravening evidence of Job's experience. It is Martha's faith as well. They do not know why God has allowed this or that temptation, trial, disaster, or pain, but the confession is the main thing: "Yes, Lord; I believe that you are the Christ, the Son of God, who is coming into the world."

Resurrection of the Loved One (11:28–44)

Mary, who had been sitting in the house, joins Martha at this point (11:28–29). Perhaps even more despondent than Martha, she who had lavished Jesus' feet with her expensive perfume has to be called out to the scene by her sister ("The Teacher is here and is calling for you"). Furthermore, upon meeting Jesus she reiterates the charge, "Lord, if you had been here, my brother would not have died" (11:32). She brings her inner struggles and anger to Jesus himself, implying that Jesus is responsible for her brother's death. It is not sin, the result of the curse, that has caused her brother's death, but Jesus' failure to respond.

To be sure, we all have a certain arrogance in thinking that, although it may well be within the rights of God's secret wisdom to give or withhold mercies in relation to others, there just couldn't be a good reason to do so in our case. Mary is not to be blamed here but to be respected for having brought her doubts, as well as her faith, to the Savior.

Jesus' own soul now begins to be drawn into turmoil as he sees the mourners and recognizes the wake that death leaves. Suddenly, he finds himself to be one of the mourners. Here he is not simply a miracle worker, who walks on the sea and calms the storms, but a man who is suddenly overtaken by troubled emotions. His own love for Lazarus and his hatred for death overwhelms him, even though he knows what he is about to do.

It is in verses 33 – 35 that we capture a glimpse of what the writer to the Hebrews meant when he said, "Therefore [Jesus] had to be made like his brothers in every respect, so that he might become a merciful and faithful high priest in the service of God, to make propitiation for the sins of the people. For because he himself has suffered when tempted, he is able to help those who are being tempted" (Hebrews 2:17 – 18). Not only at the cross, but throughout his life, Jesus experienced the whole range of temptation to sin, unbelief, weakness, and desertion in time of trouble.

> Since then we have a great high priest who has passed through the heavens, Jesus, the Son of God, let us hold fast our confession. For we do not have a high priest who is unable to sympathize with our weaknesses, but one who in every respect has been tempted as we are, yet without sin. Let us then with confidence draw near to the throne of grace, that we may receive mercy and find grace to help in time of need.
>
> Hebrews 4:14 – 16

Here at his friend's tomb, we see Jesus' anguish of soul in the presence of sin's most gruesome banner: death. He did not come with a cheerful homily on how better off Lazarus was now that he had "slipped the bonds of earth" or "sloughed off his mortal coil," for these are pagan views that would never have been countenanced by the Hebrew mind. There was no "celebration," where mourning was considered out of place. Already emotionally unhinged by Mary's weeping at his feet, Jesus came to the tomb, and we read those two words that deserve their own verse: "Jesus wept" (John 11:35). The bystanders were not sure what to make of it. "See how he loved him!" said some. "But some of them said, 'Could not he who opened the eyes of the blind man also have kept this man from dying?'" (11:36–37).

Let us pause for a moment at the remarkable report, "Jesus wept." He overthrows the various pagan conceptions of life and death that are as prevalent in our day: stoicism and sentimentalism. Some influences are more stoic in orientation. Famous for the "stiff upper lip," the ancient Stoics believed that the best souls were those that were completely free of emotion. Stirred neither by friendship nor treachery, the Stoic aimed at perfect rest. If one depended on others, he or she would soon be disappointed. In order to avoid disappointment, one should resolve never to develop attachments, except to oneself. Utter freedom from desire would make the soul a fortress against distress. For them, as for Greek thought generally, death was a liberation from the body, which was, after all, the seat of emotion — that weak part of human nature that dragged the soul down into the messiness of the world.

Closer to the Stoics, Westerners such as myself are often astonished to the point of embarrassment to watch Jews and Palestinians mourning their dead with wails and desperate gestures. But this is the culture from which Jesus came, and he was not embarrassed by it.

Sentimentalism, as I'm using the term here, refers especially to the Romantic philosophers, poets, artists, and theologians who emphasized the heart rather than the intellect as the proper seat of human dignity. Far from resisting emotional expression, sentimentalism celebrates it. Yet, unlike the Romantic movement itself, contemporary sentimentalism in its degenerate but pervasive form seems capable of wearing only a happy heart on its sleeve.

Ironically, although sentimentalism seems like the opposite of stoicism, they share some intriguing parallels. They both seem intent on avoiding the messiness of life — particularly, the tragic aspect. They want to ignore the bad news, although their solution is different. While today's stoic realizes that to abandon negative emotions one must banish all emotions, the sentimentalist believes in admitting only the good emotions, always looking on the bright side of life.

One sympathy card I saw carried a line from Henry David Thoreau: "Every blade in the field, every leaf in the forest, lays down its life in its season as beautifully as it was taken up." Even more troubling was the maxim of my father's convalescent hospital that was unfortunately enshrined in giant tapestries that hung in various parts of the complex. With scenes from childhood to old age, walking toward a sunset, it read, "The setting of the sun is as beautiful as its rising." However well-intentioned the maxim may have been, I wondered at how offensive this must have been to many who were suffering there, as their lot was trivialized. Compare for just a moment any experience you might have had with the joy of childbirth, as family and friends stand around to celebrate this new life, with the declining years, months, and days of an elderly person. One stage is full of hope in a way that the other simply cannot be forced to be. The former is attended with high expectations for one's future, the other with talk of prolonging life in the face of eventual death. One attracts visitors, family members, and friends who cannot keep themselves from holding and doting on the little one, while the other draws visits, more often than not, out of a sense of duty.

We do not enjoy spending a lot of time with those who are suffering, especially those who are dying. At least for those closest to us, we do not mind being there for the farewell, but too often it is just too long. For both the aged sufferer and his or her family, there are just too many verses to sing. I know this firsthand from my teen years. Each Christmas, my mother would write letters to area churches, asking for groups to bring some holiday cheer to our fifteen elderly residents. The same two churches made the annual appearance, neither of them evangelical—despite the fact that most residents or their children were members of various large evangelical churches in the area. Even more difficult, especially in retrospection, was the fact that each year my parents would buy presents for the residents and write the name of their children on it, since some would not be receiving even a phone call from them. I recall a couple of instances when even elders from a big church in town had simply dropped their parent off, all the while holding up themselves and their church as "pro-life." The setting of the sun is not as beautiful as its rising, as anyone close to the end can tell us.

As yet another sign of our culture's inability to handle death, we often hear, "Death is a natural part of life." This assumes the cycle-of-life approach to reality. According to this picture, life and death are just two sides of the same coin. However, the biblical picture could not be more opposite: life everlasting was the goal of creation in the beginning, while death is the curse for human sin. Death is part of the fall imposed on humanity as a result of disobedience, not an inevitable circumstance to be taken in stride. Death stands against God, against the world, against life, against hope, against possibilities.

So now we return to Jesus as he crumbles at his friend's grave. "Then Jesus, deeply moved again, came to the tomb" (11:38). Look at Jesus' face; hear his scream here. "Deeply moved" hardly captures the emotion of the original language (see also 11:33): *embrimaomai*, meaning "to snort like a horse in anger"; *tarassō* ("troubled," 11:33), meaning "agitated, confused, disorganized, fearful, surprised," as when Herod was "troubled" by the wise men (Matthew 2:3); or when the disciples were "troubled" and "cried out for fear" when Jesus walked on the sea (Matthew 14:26 NKJV). Now it is Jesus who is thrown off his horse, as it were. The Lord of life, he by whom and for whom "all things were created, in heaven and on earth, visible and invisible, whether thrones or dominions or rulers or authorities" (Colossians 1:16), now finds himself overtaken by grief. More than grief, in fact: anger. And why not? There he stands face-to-face with "the last enemy" he would defeat in his crusade against Satan. And he "wept."

The marvel in this scene is that Jesus responds in this way, even though he knows he will shortly raise Lazarus from the dead. One would expect his countenance to reveal a knowing grin that invites the crowd to anticipate his miracle. But all it shows is anguish. How much more are we allowed to weep when such an interval exists between the death of loved ones and the final resurrection! Theologically, it is the appropriate response to death—not simply because of our own sense of loss or our mourning for the survivors who are dear to us, but because of the loss to the beloved who has died. We do not grieve "as others do who have no hope" (1 Thessalonians 4:13), but we do grieve. Death is not a benign passageway to happiness but a horrible enemy attempting to keep us in the grave. Death's sting has been removed, but its bite remains. It does not have the last word for believers, but it remains the believer's antagonist until the resurrection of the body.

The good news is never that one has died, but that death has been ultimately conquered by the Lord of life. At the graveside, neither optimism nor pessimism; sentimentalism nor stoicism, tell us what is happening here. Only Jesus' cross and resurrection define the event for us.

Martha trusted Jesus when she had the stone moved at his command. Perhaps she had even heard and recalled Jesus' promise, "for the hour is coming in which all who are in the graves will hear His voice and come forth" (John 5:28–29 NKJV). The resurrection of Lazarus was in a sense a prelude to that great resurrection to come. It is *eschatological*, as are all the signs that Jesus performs. "Eschatological" is just a fancy term for the *inbreaking* of the last day, the future heavenly reality anticipated in flashes here and there even in this present age of sin and death. This resurrection of Lazarus is really not about Lazarus but about the resurrection of Jesus that it prefigures and even introduces as a foretaste. Jesus' death, burial, and resurrection is the sun that casts its shadows on this event in Bethany. This is the climactic sign, because "the last enemy to be destroyed is death" (1 Corinthians 15:26).

The response of the onlookers at this momentous scene is typical of the reaction not only to Jesus' preaching about himself but that of the apostles recorded in Acts. As with all the preaching and signs in the Scriptures and since, the effect is division. "Many ... believed" (John 11:45), but many others sought to kill Jesus. The stakes were higher. It shows that it is not for a lack of evidence that the religious leaders did not believe in Jesus. They hated him precisely to the degree that he fulfilled his messianic mission:

> *In him was life, and the life was the light of men. The light shines in the darkness, and the darkness has not overcome it....*
>
> *He was in the world, and the world was made through him, yet the world did not know him. He came to his own, and his own people did not receive him. But to all who did receive him, who believed in his name, he gave the right to become children of God, who were born,*

not of blood nor of the will of the flesh nor of the will of man, but of God.

John 1:4–5, 10–13

No More Sting

The good news in all of this is that "the *last* enemy to be destroyed is death." This means Jesus accomplished everything in his mission on earth for our complete redemption and glorification.

Death is not a portal to life. Death is not a benign friend, but a dreaded foe. It is not a natural part of life, but the most unnatural part of life you could imagine. But in *his* death and resurrection, Jesus crushed the serpent's head, vanquishing the "last enemy" of every believer. This last enemy will one day be overcome for believers in the final resurrection of the dead, but this is because it has already objectively been vanquished in the resurrection of our living Head. The resurrection of the dead on the last day has already begun on Easter morning. He is "the firstfruits of those who have fallen asleep," says the apostle (1 Corinthians 15:20).

In fact, as theologian Richard Gaffin Jr. reminds us, such organic imagery leads us to consider the resurrection of Christ and of his body as one event in two stages rather than as two separate resurrections. The firstfruits do not represent a different harvest but the beginning of the whole harvest.[1] Look at him and see what the whole harvest will be like in the end! In Christ, the end has already begun. The Head will not live without his body. The shape of the future is already present.

Lazarus was raised, but he later died. His body, raised for a time, continued where it left off in its gradual surrender to decay and death. One day, mourners would gather again at Lazarus's tomb, but this time with no expectation of resurrection—until the last day. And yet, precisely because of that confidence, precisely because Lazarus's next funeral occurred this side of Easter, they would not mourn that day as those who have no hope. After all, word would have reached them by then—perhaps some of them had even been witnesses—of the greater resurrection of Jesus himself, which would take a stand against death on its own territory, so that those united to him by faith will not remain dead. Their bodies will be raised to worship in God's renewed sanctuary.

Death is still an enemy, not a friend, but it is "the last enemy"; and it is already defeated, so that now death is not God's judgment on us for our sin but the temporal effects of our participation in Adam's guilt. Because the guilt and judgment are removed, we can both cry out with our Lord in troubled anger at death and yet also sing with the apostle, "O Death, where is your sting? O Hades, where is your victory?" (1 Corinthians 15:55 NKJV). Jesus has met the last enemy on his own turf and has entered paradise with captives in his train (Ephesians 4:8). Christ is risen indeed! Let us rejoice in that hope even with our troubled hearts and wait patiently for that greater exodus when, together with us, all of creation will sing the Song of Moses:

> *I will sing to the LORD, for he has triumphed gloriously;*
> *the horse and his rider he has thrown into the sea.*
> *The LORD is my strength and my song,*
> *and he has become my salvation;*
> *this is my God, and I will praise him,*
> *my father's God, and I will exalt him.*
> *The LORD is a man of war;*
> *the LORD is his name.*

Exodus 15:1–3

notes

chapter two: good news for losers

The epigraph to this chapter is drawn from Friedrich Nietzsche, *The Will to Power*, ed. Walter Kaufmann (New York: Vintage, 1967), 96, 542–43.

1. Cited in William E. Brown, "Rich and Smart," *World* 13 (November 14, 1998): 33.
2. Garry Wills, *Reagan's America* (New York: Penguin, 1998), 235.
3. See C. S. Lewis, *The Weight of Glory* (New York: Macmillan, 1949), 2.
4. Lyle Schaller, "From Worship to Celebration," *Worship Leader* (April–May 1993), 7.
5. Karl Barth, *The Göttingen Dogmatics: Instruction in the Christian Religion*, ed. Hannelotte Reiffen, trans. G. W. Bromiley (Grand Rapids: Eerdmans, 1991), 1:33.

chapter four: is your god big enough?

1. Quotations taken from William James, *Pragmatism and Four Essays from "The Meaning of Truth"* (New York: Meridian, 1955), 195, 192–93.
2. See Christian Smith and Melinda Lundquist Denton, *Soul Searching: The Religious and Spiritual Lives of America's Teenagers* (New York: Oxford Univ. Press, 2005).

3. Marsha G. Witten, *All Is Forgiven: The Secular Message in American Protestantism* (Princeton, N.J.: Princeton Univ. Press, 1993).

4. Clark Pinnock et al., *The Openness of God: A Biblical Challenge to the Traditional Understanding of God* (Downers Grove, Ill.: InterVarsity, 1994), 7–8.

5. C. S. Lewis, *Miracles* (New York: Macmillan, 1947), 93–94.

6. Hans Küng, *Credo: The Apostles' Creed Explained for Today* (New York: Doubleday, 1993), 86.

7. Ibid., 87.

chapter five: is anybody up there?

1. Friedrich Nietzsche, *The Will to Power*, ed. Walter Kaufmann (New York: Vintage, 1967), 542.

2. Friedrich Nietzsche, *The Gay Science*, trans. Walter Kaufmann (New York: Vintage, 1974), 125.

3. Ludwig Feuerbach, *The Essence of Christianity*, ed. E. Graham Waring and F. W. Strothmann (New York: Ungar, 1957), 47.

4. Friedrich Nietzsche, *Human, All Too Human*, trans. R. J. Hollingdale (Cambridge: Cambridge Univ. Press, 1990), 9.

5. John Calvin, *Institutes of the Christian Religion*, ed. John T. McNeill, trans. Ford Lewis Battles (Philadelphia: Westminster, 1960).

6. Calvin, *Institutes of the Christian Religion*, 3.21.1.

7. Ludwig Feuerbach, *The Essence of Christianity*, ed. E. Graham Waring and F. W. Strothmann (New York: Ungar, 1957), 16.

chapter six: if we just knew why God let it happen

1. Jim Stewart, "Religions Try to Explain Tsunamis," (CBSNEWS.com, January 6, 2005); can be viewed at www.cbsnews.com/stories/2005/01/06/eveningnews/main665307.shtml.

2. C. Everett Koop, "Faith Healing and the Sovereignty of God," in *The Agony of Deceit*, ed. Michael Horton (Chicago: Moody Press, 1990).

3. John Calvin, *Institutes of the Christian Religion*, ed. John T. McNeill, trans. Ford Lewis Battles (Philadelphia: Westminster, 1960), 1.16.9.

4. Ibid., 1.14.1.
5. John Murray, *The Collected Writings of John Murray* (Edinburgh: Banner of Truth, 1977), 2:94.
6. Ibid., 2:102.
7. Ibid.
8. Calvin, *Institutes*, 2.2.15.
9. Ibid., 4.20.14.
10. Ibid., 4.20.16.
11. Ibid., 1.17.1.
12. Ibid., 1.17.2.
13. Ibid., 1.17.4.
14. Ibid., 1.17.9.
15. Ibid., 1.16.2.

chapter eight: a new creation

1. Maureen O'Hara and Walter Truett Anderson, "Psychotherapy's Own Identity Crisis," in *The Truth about the Truth: De-confusing and Re-constructing the Postmodern World*, ed. Walter Truett Anderson (New York: Putnam, 1995), 170.
2. Ibid.
3. See Robert Jay Lifton, "The Protean Style," in *The Truth about the Truth*, 130–35.

chapter nine: the true nature of spiritual warfare

1. John Owen, *The Works of John Owen: The Nature, Power, Deceit, and Prevalency of the Remainders of Indwelling Sin in Believers*, ed. William H. Goold (Edinburgh: Banner of Truth, 1967), VI:181.

chapter ten: when god goes to a funeral

1. See Richard Gaffin Jr., *Resurrection and Redemption* (2d ed.; Phillipsburg, N.J.: Presbyterian & Reformed, 1987), especially pages 34–36.

We want to hear from you. Please send your comments about this
book to us in care of zreview@zondervan.com. Thank you.

GRAND RAPIDS, MICHIGAN 49530 USA

ZONDERVAN.COM/
AUTHORTRACKER